Brain Mystery Light and Dark

"*Brain Mystery* is an exciting tour with tentative answers of these ultimate questions that thinking human beings have been asking since the beginning of time . . . I've been enlightened by the ideas, facts, and commentaries of the many thinkers from many fields that Keyes has assembled – ancient myths, Bible stories, philosophical issues and systems, theological arguments – plus neuroscience observations and theories."

George Adelman, Visiting Scientist, MIT

In *Brain Mystery Light and Dark*, Charles Don Keyes argues that all mental states are brain events; that the notion of having a soul *is* compatible with the concept of scientific naturalism. Though most of believe that neurobiological explanations of consciousness impoverish the notion of spirituality, Keyes strongly argues why and how this *isn't* the case.

In this unique and ambitious work, Keyes draws from the neuroscientist Paul MacLean's triune brain hypothesis and Immanuel Kant's philosophical distinction between scientific and symbolic types of knowledge. *Brain Mystery* discusses the difficulty human beings sometimes have symbolizing the fragile nature of the brain. We see that symbols also express the spiritual dimension of life. Neurobiological explanations of the aesthetic, religious, and ethical symbols emphasize and reinforce their importance, as opposed to diminishing them, as is commonly thought. Don Keyes shows us that the belief in the brain/mind unity does not invalidate aesthetic, religious, and ethical symbols.

Brain Mystery Light and Dark bridges the gap between science and the humanities, and speaks especially to those who believe that both are indispensable. Those interested in neuroscience, brain evolution, and consciousness will be drawn to this extraordinary exploration.

Charles Don Keyes is a Professor of Philosophy at Duquesne University in Pittsburgh. He is the author of several books including *Foundations for an Ethic of Dignity, Four Types of Value Destruction* and *God or Ichabod?*

Brain Mystery Light and Dark

The rhythm and harmony of consciousness

Charles Don Keyes

London and New York

First published 1999
by Routledge
11 New Fetter Lane, London EC4P 4EE

Simultaneously published in the USA and Canada
by Routledge
29 West 35th Street, New York, NY 10001

© 1999 Charles Don Keyes

Typeset in Palatino by RefineCatch Limited, Bungay, Suffolk
Printed and bound in Great Britain by
Biddles Ltd, Guildford and King's Lynn

British Library Cataloguing in Publication Data
A catalogue record for this book is available from the British Library

Library of Congress Cataloguing in Publication Data
Keyes, C. D. (Charles Don)
    Brain mystery light and dark : the rhythm and harmony of
    consciousness / Charles Don Keyes.
Includes bibliographical references and index.
    1. Consciousness.   2. Brain.   I. Title.
    B808.9.K49   1999
126 – dc21   98–16983

ISBN 0–415–18050–3 (hbk)
ISBN 0–415–18051–1 (pbk)

In memory of those members of my family – father,
Robert Keyes, MD; mother, Ruth Brown Keyes; brother,
William Robert Keyes; and maternal grandmother,
Ollie Chaney Brown – with whom I lived in the house
where I first asked the questions of this book.

Contents

Preface

Brain Mystery Light and Dark is the outcome of a struggle that started more than half a century ago when I first asked how the brain becomes conscious. I persisted in asking that question through the decades in which it was not fashionable until, at the end of the century, consciousness has thankfully become a subject of intense scientific interest. The Epilogue gives an account of the events that forced me to start reflecting on the relation between brain and mind. So that the arguments of the intervening chapters can be evaluated in their own right apart from their autobiographical origins, the Epilogue ought to be read last.

This book has four basic theses: First, brain events and mental states are two sides of the same undivided unity. This monistic position does not eliminate consciousness, but attests to its reality as the subjective dimension of neurobiological processes. Second, the question of how the brain becomes consciousness *is* answerable in principle, contrary to what some claim. This is a scientific, not a philosophical, question, since consciousness is an event of nature and therefore must be explained in terms of physical causality. Third, the scientific naturalism of the first two theses, contrary to what many mistakenly take for granted, does not deny the spiritual dimension of life (aesthetics, religion, ethics). Fourth, the tragic vulnerability of the human brain creates problems that only the spiritual dimension can resolve.

Immanuel Kant's distinction between scientific experience and aesthetic judgment in the *Critique of Judgement* is the theory of knowledge at the base of this book. Scientific knowledge is empirical and aesthetic knowledge symbolic. The brain/mind unity apprehends the beautiful and sublime in aesthetic and religious experience symbolically. It generates ethical thoughts, feelings, and actions. Ethical value can stand independently of religion.

The scientific nature of questions about the origin of consciousness does not prevent philosophy from interpreting what they mean in relation to a wide range of human experiences. Philosophical theories are also capable of integrating different scientific models of consciousness and possibly suggesting new areas for empirical investigation. This book is not bound by conventional stereotypes of philosophical conflict. On the one hand, it safeguards the unity of brain/ mind without undermining the validity of subjective states. On the other hand, it synthesizes a conceptually and historically wide range of sources commonly held to be incompatible with that kind of monism. The prime instance is its retrieving Plato's good, the just, and the fair from his body/soul dualism, as well as restating his theory of the rhythm and harmony of music as neurobiological processes.

Paul D. MacLean's triune brain concept plays an inadvertent but important role in the naturalistic recasting of Plato. The following chapters also give new information about MacLean's controversial and extremely pervasive concept in the light of his most recent definitive publications and extensive private interviews, thereby challenging earlier misconstructions based on incomplete information about his project as a whole. The triune brain concept, thus reinterpreted, is a point of departure throughout much of the book and also one of its main gadflies. This book also discusses a number of other neuroscientific studies, especially those that include self-referent models of consciousness.

The brain's dark mystery is its tragic vulnerability and also the odd kind of trouble it seems to have referring to itself. Still another side of the dark mystique is the way in which the brain, the most advanced product of evolution on earth, produces injustice and all manner of other evils. These are not the legacy of our animal past but a kind of bestiality peculiar to nature's masterpiece. The bright mystery of the brain includes the fact that the same evolutionary masterpiece is also capable of attributing ultimate importance to the good, the just, and the fair.

Pittsburgh
17 October 1997

Acknowledgments

Scientists and other scholars made indispensable contributions to my research. Paul D. MacLean is the most notable. He gave considerable time to me during several visits to his laboratory, read and criticized manuscript, corresponded with me, and referred me to other helpful contributors. These include Steven Peterson, James Ashbrook, Brian Cooney, and Rodney Holmes. Private consultations, some extensive, with each of them, greatly enhanced the scope of my research, and so have telephone conversations and correspondence with George Adelman. I thank Michael J. Katz who initiated all of this by referring me to Dr MacLean, and Mary Mahowold for referring me to Dr Katz during the late 1980s.

Duquesne University provided money for travel during the spring of 1990, without which it would have been impossible to carry through with this chain of referrals. I thank Eleanore Holveck, departmental chair, for her constant support and encouragement. The university provided a starter grant during the summer of 1991 and since then has sponsored travel to conferences where I have presented papers related to the writing of the manuscript. These include the Greater Philadelphia Philosophy Consortium, Institute of Liberal Studies (Kentucky State University), Society for the Scientific Study of Sex (Chicago), and partial subsidy of travel to Star Island, New Hampshire, for the 41st Annual Conference of the Institute on Religion in an Age of Science, where I presented an early version of material in this book.

I thank *Zygon: Journal of Religion & Science* for allowing me to subsume my Star Island presentation, which they had published as an article, into this book. The *Journal of Social and Evolutionary Systems* gave me similar permission to use material closely related to an article I had published with them. East Central University of Oklahoma sent and allowed me to use photographs of the Callixylon tree and science hall. George Back gave permission to quote from his newsletter about the bombing of the federal building in Oklahoma City. An anonymous person, fictitiously named "Dan," has allowed me to publish his lamentation and nightmare in Chapters 7 and 8.

Four Duquesne University students deserve special thanks for their help and encouragement as the end of the project approached: Matthew Morgan offered critical comments on several versions, prepared the bibliography, verified references, and assisted in requesting permissions; Havah Armstrong made extensive typographical adjustments and made helpful editorial comments; Patricia Carnevalli gave essential editorial advice; and Ryan Walther made the index and helped with the page proofs. At an earlier time, two other students, Christopher Nagel and Jennifer Boyce, gave valuable editorial advice while they helped me type the manuscript. I thank Joan Thompson, departmental secretary, and numerous student aides for their care and patient help at all stages of the project, especially those who helped me struggle to meet deadlines: Patty Cain, Allison Bralich, and Tina Adams.

Other individuals deserve thanks for contributions that cannot be stated simply. Rebecca Demas gave extraordinary editorial advice and encouragement, both at the beginning of the writing and again at the end. She invented the book's title. I quote some of her criticisms as those of the "perceptive critic" in certain parts of the manuscript. She helped me articulate its conceptual structure.

Hiroko Kiifner, in about 1989, read early versions of the autobiographical material that turned out to be the Epilogue when I mistakenly thought it would be the first chapter of the book. I thank her for suggesting that I turn the continuation, which I had not yet written, into a book for university students, thereby helping me to start writing it. Lois D. Hurt gave advice that helped me finish the last few unwritten pages of Chapter 6 during August of 1997. I especially thank those who gave indispensable help as I prepared the final revision during January and February of 1998. Patricia Devine provided counsel that freed me to devise a revision plan. Patricia Carnevali assisted me with all aspects of the revision itself.

Joseph Pawlosky (Assistant Professor of English, East Central University, Ada, Oklahoma), starting in 1989, also read several versions of the material that became the Epilogue. He took a special interest in my manuscript because it reports events that happened on and near his campus during and after the Second World War. He gave advice that helped me develop the nascent manuscript. Like Hiroko Kiifner, the literary agent, he encouraged me to start writing it. Like Rebecca Demas, the psychologist, he also returned to help me at the end. In his extraordinary ability as a fiction writer, he enabled me to cope with factual and sometimes disturbing autobiographical confessions. Professor Pawlosky therefore bears the title of official editor of the beginning and end of the book. He edited the Epilogue in exceedingly subtle ways, preserving my own language and structure throughout. He edited the brief Prologue more aggressively, intervening there to help me state what I could not otherwise articulate.

Callixylon tree

Edited by Joseph Pawlosky

The story starts here, on the front porch of my boyhood home in Ada, Oklahoma. Looking one block to the east from this porch, I am able to take in, each time I leave and enter the house, at a single glance two historically significant monuments situated prominently at the entrance of the campus of East Central State College, now East Central University. In a curious way, though now some thousand miles distant, it is as if I never left that porch, considering how I am able, these 50-some years later, to take in at a single glance of my mind's eye the formative role played by those two markers and their underlying significance in my life's quest to come to grips with the human brain and its mysterious workings. From my earliest encounter with those two fixtures, one of them the rugged, 8-foot high remains of a fossilized tree, the other a pair of memorial pillars standing sentry at the gateway to the campus, it now seems clear that the first pages of this book were, in those preschool years, already being written, though I could hardly have known it at the time. There may indeed be something here of Martin Heidegger's observation that "origin always comes to meet us from the future" (Heidegger 1971 [1959]: 10).

Those two markers, however, besides symbolizing, indeed, in a certain way even effecting, the direction of my life's interest in, and study of, the brain, represent as well certain epochal milestones in the history of the human species. The first marker, the massive, craggy, reconstructed remains of a fossilized Callixylon tree (Figure 1) some 250 million years old, stands in stark contrast to the stately pillars of the memorial gate dedicated to the memory of those students killed in the First World War. Like quaintly mismatched bookends, the pillars and the fossilized tree situated side by side reflect something of the earliest, as well as the most recent, chapters in the story of human life on the planet.

For whatever unknown reason, the Choctaw Indian who first unearthed the several tons of stony remains of the Callixylon tree on his pig farm in Pontotoc County, near the town of Ada, seems to have sensed something of their importance. Why he would have kept digging when their exact nature would have been opaque to him is not possible to know,

Figure 1 Callixylon tree (East Central University photograph)

but he did not stop until he had exhumed the entire cache of the heavy fragments, leaving them scattered on the ground, there for scientists eventually to be summoned to examine and identify some years later. Subsequently, East Central students would laboriously transport the many tons of fragments to the campus, where they came to be set into a trunk-shaped bed of concrete and formally dedicated on 22 March 1936. There they stand today, in some approximate guise of their former appearance, some 250 million years ago.

The war memorial, constituted of twin, square, 12-foot limestone pillars flanking the campus's main entrance, impose a solemnity of its own with the winged extension of each pillar seeming to embrace any who would approach. These two structures, the Callixylon tree and the war memorial, together stand in arresting testimony to the duration of our species, as well as to the quantitative insignificance of our tragedy, bespeaking the singular human capacity for compassion, though compassion as often as not called forth by suffering inflicted through the agency of our own inspired barbarity, with both in ample evidence over the vast stretch of evolutionary time. Life's history, coursing through the slow process of natural selection as etched into the craggy fragments of the Callixylon, is a biological narrative of great magnitude, just as our race's history, spanning the millennia of recorded and unrecorded time, is a dramatic narrative that continues even now to unfold with such scenes of grandeur and misery as betoken the human condition.

Paul MacLean, MD, senior research scientist at the National Institute of Mental Health, has contributed significantly to *Brain Mystery Light and Dark*, and he speaks of both the misery and the grandeur of the human story. MacLean's accounting for the simultaneous dark and light sides of our nature is rooted in his hypothesis that the present human brain has retained the earlier stages of its evolutionary development:

> Man, it appears, has inherited essentially three brains. Frugal Nature in developing her paragon threw nothing away. The oldest of his brains is basically reptilian; the second has been inherited from lower animals; and the third and newest brain is a late mammalian development which reaches a pinnacle in man and gives him his unique power of symbolic language.
>
> (MacLean 1964: 96)

The reptilian brain in us is the "R-complex;" our "lower animal" (paleomammalian) heritage is the limbic system; whilst the newest of the human brain's mammalian (neomammalian) structures are the prefrontal areas of the neocortex. Since the three brains function as one, MacLean represents the human brain as being "triune."

So complex an organ would hardly have appeared in an instant, given Nature's characteristically deliberate manner of working things out. More like aeons than mere millennia would have been required for such development, aeons seeping from farther back in time than even the Permian Age subscribed to by MacLean as marking the coalescence of the three brains into one, aeons that one finds captured so strikingly by few remnants on this planet as the fossilized remains of a 250-million-year-old tree trunk. But whether of such antiquity, or, on the other hand, of such recentness as a twentieth-century war memorial, the reflection we catch upon examination of such artifacts turns out to be none but that of the examiner himself. What fastens our attention is not that it is ourselves that we see, but rather that our seeing self would actually recognize what it beholds, that it would in some manner know, in gazing into its own eyes, that it knows.

Part one

Shadow journey

Paul D. MacLean's foremost critic, John Durant, claims that the triune brain concept is "probably the single, most-influential idea in brain science in the postwar period, at least in terms of public or popular perceptions as for what brain science has to say about the human condition" (Durant 1992: 268). Chapter 2 introduces MacLean's concept, examines Durant's criticism of it, and reinterprets it as an inadvertent naturalistic restatement of Plato's "triune" metaphor of the soul as a "many-headed, many colored beast" in Book 9 of the *Republic*. The same metaphor can also describe both the misery and grandeur of the human condition, respectively the strife of injustice and the harmony of justice.

I argue that mental states are brain events. This position opposes theories that claim that body (brain) and soul (mental states) are two different kinds of substance, including the Platonic split between the two and similar dualistic theories. At the same time, reduction of mind to brain does not eliminate mental states or suggest that they are unimportant, as some claim. On the contrary, aesthetic, religious, and ethical symbols are real partly *because* they are brain events. Chapter 1 journeys beyond the destruction of Platonic dualism to find the core of Plato's philosophy which can be retrieved from its discarded dualistic container. Music is the most important part of the core.

Plato likens the human condition to that of prisoners in an underground dungeon chained so that they cannot see actual objects, but only shadows on the wall cast by the light of a fire burning behind them. One of the prisoners, freed of his chains, to his amazement sees the objects that cause the reflection. These underground objects and their shadows stand for actual sense perceptions.

He resists liberation from the dungeon, but someone above ground drags him out into the sunlight which initially overwhelms and temporarily blinds him until he begins to regain his sight by degrees. At first he cannot see things above ground directly, but only their reflections ("shadows," "phantoms") in water. Later he sees the "things themselves" that cause these reflections and finally can look directly at the sun (Plato 1968: 516A–B). The sun stands for the good, source of the "things themselves," namely the forms (or ideas, the "really real") like the fair and the just. Mathematical entities reflect the forms, and the allegory represents them as the reflections in water.

Some current neurobiolgical models of consciousness attach importance to the theory Plato illustrates by the allegory of the cave. Chapter 6 refers to two such suggestions. Roger Penrose asks whether the Platonic forms might actually exist as the ground of mathematics. Bernard Barrs suggests that Plato's image of "fire-cast shadows" refers to some biologically generated "spotlight of attention" that might be the source of consciousness (Baars 1997: 5). Suggestions like these are evidence that late twentieth-century natural science has become dissatisfied with positivistic restrictions.

Chapters 1 and 2 recast essential parts of Plato's idealism in a naturalistic mode. They are a shadow journey in the positive sense that they focus on music as the privileged type of sense perception. Auditory shadows of musical rhythm and harmony might be the most direct route to mathematical entities and whatever they might reflect. It is interesting that Plato has Socrates ask: "Do you want to see ugly things, blind and crooked, when it's possible to hear bright and fair ones from others?" (Plato 1968: 506C–D).

Music is also the Platonic fortress that remains steadfast and untouched after the destruction of dualism. It is the guardhouse within the guardian part of us, the seat of courage. Music consists of three parts: words, rhythm, and harmony. The words of music, however, are subordinate to rhythm and harmony, which are sovereign. The poetic plots that words narrate arise from still more basic rhythms and harmonies of consciousness and can be resolved into them. We witness both the destruction of dualism and recovery of the fortress by a certain way of reading the *Phaedo*, Plato's account of Socrates' attempt the night before he was executed to prove that the soul survives death.

Chapter 1

The fortress

Death is one of two things, according to Socrates, and neither is to be feared. It is total annihilation, an eternal sleep without dreams, or else it is a journey to another place. That was Socrates' answer to the death sentence in the *Apology*.

Plato's *Phaedo*

At his execution, Socrates holds fast to the second of these possibilities: "Does not death mean that the body comes to exist by itself, separated from the soul, and the soul exists by herself, separated from the body?" (Plato 1951: 64C). The soul's eternal destiny and its present happiness now depend upon whether it lives justly or unjustly during its bodily existence. Justice is harmony and injustice is disharmony among the wisdom-loving, honor-loving, and gain-loving activities that make up the soul. These three vital functions are respectively the ruling, guardian, and producer psychological structures within individual human beings. Moderation must order and master the sensual gain-loving part that desires more food, sex, wine, and money. Courage must keep the honor-loving part that desires to score steadfast in the face of the pleasures, pains, fears, and desires that would otherwise distract it. Both of these vital functions that desire are mortal. Only the wisdom-loving "part" survives death.

The middle of the dialogue presents Socrates the philosopher struggling to prove that his wisdom-loving soul actually does survive death. Near the end, he narrates what his religious faith holds about how souls will be judged in Hades. Souls that survive the judgment pass through many reincarnations, until those that have "sufficiently purified themselves with philosophy" overcome the need for bodies and "proceed to dwellings still fairer" (Plato 1951: 114C).

The *Phaedo* is a paradox. On the one hand, it epitomizes all the subsequent western theories of immortality that it inspires: "Then, it seems, when death attacks a man, his mortal part dies, but his immortal part retreats before death, and goes away safe and indestructible" (Plato

1951: 106E). On the other hand, it is a battle-field of belief and doubt. This dialogue invites skepticism about what it affirms. Doubt plagues Socrates while the dialogue seems to invite us to get rid of the body/soul dualism that contains the belief. This skepticism expresses itself in at least three ways. The cogency of Simmias' counter-argument is the first and most obvious way. The body produces the soul, according to Simmias, and when the body dies, the product ceases to exist. Simmias' position stands between idealism and materialism. It points towards the former because he says that the soul is more divine than the body; but it is more like the latter in the sense that there are only material causes. The soul cannot go on existing when the body is dead because the soul emerges from the body in the way a musical harmony does from a lyre. Simmias says:

> It might be said that the harmony in a tuned lyre is something unseen, and incorporeal, and perfectly beautiful, and divine, while the lyre and its strings are corporeal, and with the nature of bodies, and com-pounded, and earthly, and akin to the mortal . . . when the lyre is broken and the strings are cut or snapped . . . the harmony, which is of the same nature as the divine and the immortal, and akin to them, has perished, and perished before the mortal lyre . . . . And I think, Socrates, that you too must be aware that many of us believe the soul to be most probably a mixture and harmony of the elements by which our body is, as it were, strung and held together . . . the soul, though most divine, must perish at once, like other harmonies of sound and of all works of art . . .
>
> (Plato 1951: 85E–86D)

Plato lets Socrates flounder when he tries to answer Simmias' argument that the soul is a harmony. This is a second indication of the *Phaedo's* skepticism. Socrates claims "it is quite wrong to say that the soul is a harmony" (Plato 1951: 94E) because harmony or the lack of it is a quality in souls that already exist, not the cause of their existence. By reverting to his definition of justice as harmony and injustice as disharmony, he fails to get to the bottom of Simmias' main point, which is that the soul depends upon the body for its existence. Does the fact that Plato lets Socrates equivocate about harmony and causality suggest that he is more critical of dualism than his teacher?

Socrates himself claims that at an earlier time he himself had believed that brains are the organ of consciousness. He admits this after he failed to answer Simmias' objection:

> When I was a young man, I had a passionate desire for the wisdom which is called Physical Science. I thought it a splendid thing to know the causes of everything; why a thing comes into being, and why it

perishes, and why it exists. I was always worrying myself with questions such as . . . . Is it . . . the brain which gives the senses of hearing and sight and smell . . . ?

(Plato 1951: 96B)

Clearly Socrates no longer holds this belief, but might some imprint of it be linked to his inability to deal with Simmias' objection? He might be struggling with doubts that spring from challenges to body/soul dualism.

Immediately after narrating his religious creed about the soul's survival, Socrates claims that it is worth while to stake everything on this belief:

A man of sense will not insist that these things are exactly as I have described them. But I think that he will believe that something of the kind is true of the soul and her habitations, seeing that she is shown to be immortal, and that it is worth his while to stake everything on this belief. The venture is a fair one, and he must charm his doubts with spells like these. That is why I have been prolonging the fable [*mythos*] all this time.

(Plato 1951: 114D)

Does Socrates admit that he "charms doubts" through religious myth because he is uncertain whether his arguments stand up to Simmias' criticism? Does he *wager* that he will survive death because he doubts the validity of his own proofs of immortality? If so, his need to charm his doubts now might account for his statement in the *Apology* that annihilation might follow death.

The fastest gun in the west

The human brain, supreme product of evolution, is extraordinarily fragile. Its unimaginable complexity alongside its vulnerability might partly explain why we try to deny that it is the organ of consciousness. Do our brains engage in denial because not doing so would smash protective vestiges of the soul substance illusion? Dualism is an emotional prophylactic against the cosmic threat, but monism forbids us to wear any such protective covering. Overwhelming amounts of scientific evidence show us that it is not rational to split brain and mind into two different realms of reality. Brain and mind are identical in the sense that every mental state is a neurobiological process. Monism confronts us with the fragility of our existence, the inevitability of our death, and our tragic vulnerability.

Brain/mind is even more fragile than most people think. George Wolf visited a laboratory that monitored the impulses of individual neurons by translating them into "popping" sounds. He also heard "a soft moan" and asked the researcher what it was. He told Wolf that "it was the sound of dying cell – a high frequency discharge as the cell's life ebbed away." Wolf reflects that "the moan was an expression of a feeling that all sentient creatures share – it was a feeling of perishing" (Wolf 1984: 119). How many of your own brain cells do you suppose might have "moaned" their death in the time it takes you to read this page?

An account by Vernon Mark and Frank Ervin of the damage a stroke did to the thalamus of a 43-year-old accountant shows how vulnerable the brain/mind is. What happened to him puts a fitting cap on much I share in the Epilogue:

> He was awake and alert and able to see and follow objects, and could move both his hands and feet; but he retained only one item out of his cultural past. He kept repeating over and over again the phrase, 'The fastest gun in the West,' which was all he remembered. He did not recognize his own wife and children when they came to visit him; and to their pathetic attempts to remind him who they were, he could only mumble, 'The fastest gun in the West, the fastest gun in the West.'
> (Mark and Ervin 1970: 142)

Could it be that he kept saying that because he thought someone had shot him?

Hope as meaning and purpose[1]

The fact that brain and mind are a unity clearly makes the human condition tragic, possibly absurd, since the organ of consciousness is both mortal and exceedingly vulnerable. All our thoughts, feelings, memories, and every mental state depend upon fragile neurons that are already dying. If we translate what brain/mind monism means into human terms, it turns into a crisis (Part four) resembling what Paul Tillich calls the despair of meaninglessness. Also following Tillich, I am going to conclude that "The act of accepting meaninglessness is in itself a meaningful act" (Tillich 1952: 176). Accepting despair, however, is not giving in to it, but spiting it by getting on top of despair and wrestling with it. This activity is courage.

Resolving the crisis requires a kind of courage that is consistent with scientific evidence and also does not undermine the spiritual dimension of life. This dimension is not a substance but a process in which brain/mind attributes ultimate importance to aesthetic, religious, and ethical symbols (Part five). Neuroscience rightly asks how the brain produces such processes, even though their meaning is beyond the limits of scientific judgment. The spiritual dimension of life gives hope in spite of the crisis of monism. Elsewhere I define hope within the limits of our bodily existence as the "*simultaneous possession of meaning*, which is the participation in value bestowing symbols, *and purpose*, which is the projection of meaningful possibilities and goals into the future and thereby sensing time's continuity between them and the present" (Keyes 1989: 1). Hope is both mystical and practical. Its roots are aesthetic.

Science and aesthetics

Immanuel Kant distinguishes between scientific and aesthetic intuitions and establishes the legitimacy of both in their difference in the *Critique of Judgement*. This decisive work that he thinks completes his system goes entirely beyond the spiritual narrowness of much eighteenth-century thought. He shows that science and aesthetics use (present) categories (concepts) like causality and substance in two different ways.

Scientific knowledge presents categories directly, not figuratively. It uses language in a literal (demonstrative) way and is strictly limited to factual information (sensible intuitions). This would, of course, include empirically testable hypotheses. When we use categories scientifically in these ways according to our experience of nature, Kant calls them *schemata*: "The schema is, properly, only the phenomenon, or sensible concept, of an object in agreement with the category" (Kant 1965 [1787]: B 186).

Aesthetic knowledge, by contrast, uses categories indirectly as *symbols*, namely by a "double function." It takes an object of "sensible intuition" and "reflects" (bends back) on it analogically. Kant uses the mundane example of a hand mill as symbolizing a despotic state: "For between a despotic state and a hand mill there is, to be sure, no similarity; but there is a similarity in the rules according to which we reflect upon things and their causality." Similarly, but more profoundly, aesthetic intuition and the feelings of the beautiful and the sublime that characterize it, as well as the language required to express it, are "symbolical." Ethics is aesthetically significant since "the beautiful is the symbol of the morally good." Religious faith depends upon a sublime aesthetic intuition, since "all our knowledge of God is merely symbolical" (Kant 1968 [1790]: Sec. 59). The meaning of symbols cannot be tested empirically, but this does not make them arbitrary as the many suppose, since (as Part five shows) we can describe them with rigor and practical cogency and state scientific hypotheses about their neurobiological origins.

Solipsism and reality

The brain is not directly conscious of sense experience, because the sense organs and complex translation processes lie between events in the outside world and our awareness of them. As a result, some speculation about neuroscience and about Kant's position or both tends to doubt that the outside world exists. This position is called solipsism. It literally means that only the self exists, but here it implies that only the brain does. But the suspicion that there are no things-in-themselves out there and that the brain is the source of the sensations is a philosophical elaboration essentially alien to Kant's position. Solipsism is the supreme unwarranted hypothesis. Scientific and aesthetic experience attest to this because they both validate knowledge through a dialectic that requires human interplay.

Science is also essentially anti-solipsistic because it seeks empirical knowledge. By its very nature, neuroscience studies the brain events that mediate our perceptions, not the external sources from which they come. The methodological focus resembles solipsism only by faulty analogy. Manifestly, neuroscientists presume that the brains (other than their own) they study actually exist. Francis Crick correctly hypothesizes that

> there is indeed an outside world, and that it is largely independent of our observing it. We can never fully know this outside world, but we can obtain approximate information about some aspects of its properties by using our senses and the operations of our brains.
>
> (Crick 1995: 12)

Aesthetics also shuns solipsism. The fine arts are essentially immersed in reality. What we sense, not merely that we sense, matters. Music instantiates this. Rhythm and harmony are neurobiological processes, but they also come from outside the brain. Music also has external status in the sense that we can hear somebody else playing it and play it for others. We debate with them about it, analyze it mathematically, and study it historically. Music can enflame passion and communicate private feelings, even without words. It can produce social unity or subvert it.

External reality produces effects on brain function, and brain function changes affect external reality. Events in the outside world are sources of misery and happiness, partly because of what our brains make of them, and partly because of what they are in and of themselves. For example, hope aesthetically volitilizes practical activity. Its purposefulness awakens consciousness from the nightmare of being trapped in a solipsistic cocoon, aims at a goal, goes forth, and grabs hold of it. Hope responds to reality, deconstructs it, reconstructs it, and returns to itself with something new.

Can hope fire a neuron?

Judith Hooper and Dick Teresi ask: "How can a thought, which has no mass, no electrical charge, no velocity, no material propensities, act upon a physical organ, the brain?" (Hooper and Teresi 1986: 66). They explain three widely held answers:

MATERIALIST ANSWER: It can't. Have you ever tried to slice bread with your will? Well, it's just as silly to imagine that thoughts can slip through a brain-cell membrane and invade the nucleus or can jump up and down on the axon to make it fire. Mental phenomena, being immaterial by definition, don't affect physical objects.

REDUCTIONIST ANSWER: Thoughts, schmoughts. All your thoughts are *really* just electrochemical blips in nervous tissue. Because "mental states" are ghostly by-products of brain events, mere figments, there's no need to worry about how the two might interact.

DUALIST-INTERACTIONIST ANSWER: As surely as there are tables and rocks, there are desires, beliefs, perceptions, worries, dreams, regrets, memories, and pains in the universe. Mental states are real, even if you can't see, touch, or taste them, and they do influence our brains.

(Hooper and Teresi 1986: 67)

The fact that the materialist, reductionist, and dualist–interactionist answers are all defective makes them an especially useful point of departure for seeking a scientifically sound concept of the brain/mind relation that also respects the value of life.

Materialism makes sense of substance, but it is an overly simplistic theory of what is and is not. Materialism is similar to dualism in thinking that mental states (like hope) have to be substances of some type or else they are nothing. It aims at being scientific but reveals its lack of sophistication by being too simplistic. Dualism situates mind (soul) safely beyond materialism by claiming that mind (soul) is an immaterial substance. It makes nonsense of substance by pushing it beyond nature, as in saying that intangible mental events are substances. "Immaterial substance" is a contradiction in terms. Dualism is misplaced transcendence. It rightly seeks to preserve the value of human life, but it is extravagant in the way it reacts against the simplistic exclusiveness of materialism. Scientific evidence does not support the theory that brain (body) and mind (soul) are two different kinds of substance that then interact with one another.

Neuroscientific evidence seems to require that we view brain/mind as a unity. This evidence argues against substance dualism, the theory that brain and mind (soul) are two different kinds of reality that then interact with one another. The same evidence also argues against the kind of materialism that cannot recognize the existence of mental states. The reductionist theory that all mental states are brain events fits the brain/mind unity model. The particular reductionist answer Hooper and Teresi offer, however, is defective, and its defectiveness is symptomatic of how distortions can corrode truth to the point of making it unrecognizable. This reductionism in this example does not go far enough because its claim that the "mental states" in question are "ghostly by-products" is an unfinished reduction. At the same time, this example goes too far in the direction of explaining thoughts away because they are "*really* just electrochemical blips in nervous tissue." There is a delicate balance between asserting the fact that all mental events are brain products and the distorted claim that they are unimportant since they are nothing but brain events.

Eliminative reduction

Behaviorism, according to John B. Watson, eliminates "all subjective terms such as sensation, perception, image, desire, purpose, and even thinking and emotion as they were subjectively defined" (Watson 1924: 6). Even though this barbaric kind of eliminative reduction died as a psychological theory, its ghost still haunts some current attempts to eliminate subjective states like those on Watson's list. For instance, Patricia Churchland's search for "the conceptual framework of a matured neuroscience," which she calls "eliminative materialism," would eliminate "folk psychology." This "sentimental" and "intuitive" way of explaining behavior focuses especially on "*belief* and *desire*" as well as other commonsense "crinkum-crankum" such as "perceptions, expectations, goals, sensations, and so forth" (Churchland 1986: 396).

It helps to remember that all such eliminative positions are philosophical theories. The supposed necessity for their interpretative perspective is neither contained in nor integral to the scientific evidence. Eliminative reductionism is a defective interpretation because the mental states it denies manifestly exist. We know they are real because we actually experience them, but this does not mean that mental states are properties that emerge from the brain like ghostly by-products.

Astonishing hypothesis

Crick's "astonishing hypothesis," which builds partly on Patricia Churchland's position and overcomes some of its limitations, helps clarify neurobiological reduction. It claims that "'You,' your joys and your sorrows, your memories and your ambitions, your sense of personal identity, your sense of free will, are in fact no more than the behavior of a vast assembly of nerve cells and their associated molecules" (Crick 1995: 3).

This kind of reduction largely avoids the two excesses of Hooper and Teresi's specimen. On the one hand, his astonishing hypothesis accounts for the brain's emergent behavior without turning it into a "ghostly by-product." On the other hand, he does not pretend it does not exist. His position does not eliminate the subjective significance of consciousness. Behavior is emergent, he argues, if it cannot be explained by merely separate parts of the brain "such as the individual neurons." It can be understood only from the "nature and behavior of its parts *plus* the knowledge of how all these parts interact." Crick's position is rational in the sense that it simultaneously opposes the behaviorist denial of consciousness and the dualist denial that the brain produces it. He is correct in claiming that the answer to the question of how the brain becomes conscious is scientific, not philosophical, precisely because it is a question about natural causality.

Why is the structure of consciousness hidden?

It is presently hidden, according to Crick, not because it is unanswerable in principle (as Colin McGinn claims[2]) but because science has not yet found the answer. Crick is correct in arguing that "the study of consciousness is a scientific problem," and he inspires hope that science will eventually answer it, since "we can now see ways of approaching the problem experimentally." His insistence that the search for an answer is only peripherally philosophical is well-founded:

> Philosophers are right in trying to discover better ways of looking at the problem and in suggesting fallacies in our present thinking. That they have made so little real progress is because they are looking at the system from the outside. That makes them use the wrong idiom.
>
> (Crick 1995: 256)

Crick: scientist and rhetorician

Crick also writes that "It has been unkindly said that a philosopher is too often a person who prefers imaginary experiments to real experiments and thinks that an explanation of a phenomenon in everyday words is all that is needed" (Crick 1995: 258). His "skewering philosophy and religion," as a reviewer quoted on the back of his book enthusiastically calls it, is rhetoric, not science. But this does not undermine the validity of his empirical research into consciousness. He writes that philosophers ought not to display "lofty superiority" about their theories, especially in view of their "poor record" in explaining consciousness, but ought to be ready to abandon their "pet theories" when proven wrong. We need to follow Crick's advice even further and recognize the danger of falling into flat intellectual provincialism, a type of inverse loftiness I am tempted to call belief in the "superiority of the surface."

Against silly reductionism: the truth is the whole

Philosophy is, among other things, the process of challenging surfaces. It must always call one-sidedness into question. Never attribute infallibility to *any* system, including your own. True philosophers are not only self-critical of their own systems, but they also *invite* rational criticism from others. (Answering satire wastes time.) Isolation does not strengthen a system or a person's commitment to it; dialogue with the truest version of its opposite does. An authentic dialogue aims not at scoring, but at learning through criticism.

Philosophers must be as critical of other philosophers' mistakes as they are of their own. Such mistakes include, but are not limited to, claiming that something is an empirical fact when it is not. Aristotle, for instance, said that the brain's function is to cool blood. At the same time, anyone with even a smidgen of rationality would challenge the simplistic cliché that a system, in this case Aristotle's, is invalid if the philosopher makes a mistake. Respect for reason also means having the historical perspective to see that Aristotle's system has contributed significantly to the advance of the scientific method and consequently of the ability not to mistake brains for blood coolers.

We have to overcome narrowness to be constructively critical, grow through dialogue, and challenge simplistic clichés that are often concealed with seeming sophistication. This grievous vice thrives on time-bound provincialism, confinement to the present moment of intellectual time, pride in amnesia about the ongoing history of ideas. The same vice manifests itself in refusing to get inside primary texts of a wide range of systems from various historical epochs.

Written western philosophy alone consists of many intellectual traditions that share a common belief in truth but have different views of what it is. For instance, the differences extend from empiricism to idealism, from systems expressed in metaphysical language to positivism's critique of it. Today, as always, a particular philosopher stands somewhere with respect to these or other spectrums or some combination of them. A *real philosopher*, however, recognizes the truth claim she or he makes by standing somewhere in a particular philosophical context, whilst also recognizing that this is one of many possible contexts and respecting the whole of which one's own is a part. Crick's excursions into philosophy would be sounder if he based them on a broader grasp of this historic whole. I agree with him, nevertheless, that philosophers must abandon and not pet all or any one of my theories the moment they are proven wrong.

Keeping that in mind, I propose this theory: Consciousness is paradoxical if we measure it by the rules that regulate ordinary concepts. For instance, mind is both different from brain and identical with it. McGinn knows there is some natural structure that "converts brain 'gook'" into consciousness, but the conversion seems so radically paradoxical that he thinks the properties responsible for it "belong to the hidden nature of consciousness" (McGinn 1991: 100). He errs when he gives up the quest for a scientific answer, but the fact that he capitulates in this way attests to the uniqueness of the paradox. Crick rightly insists that science will probably explain the conversion into consciousness if it persists. However, I doubt that it will do this by using any number of ordinary empirical concepts. The answer will have to come through extraordinary empirical concepts. As philosopher, I wonder if one such extraordinary characteristic might be the capability of not always being bound by the principle of non-contradiction: "A cannot be A and not-A."

G.W.F. Hegel, philosopher of overabundance, proposes a dialectical method that defies normal thinking, just as the relation between brain and mind does. He writes that

> contradiction is the root of all movement and vitality; it is only in so far as something has a contradiction within it that it moves, has urge and activity . . . . Something is therefore alive only in so far as it contains contradiction within it, and moreover is this power to hold and endure the contradiction within it.
>
> (Hegel 1969 [1816]: 439–40)

Hegel's dialectical method is applicable to the brain/mind problem partly because it can simultaneously suspend and affirm contradictions. His philosophy is mainly concerned with "determinations quite different from those in ordinary . . . so-called common sense" (Hegel 1969 [1816]: 84). Parts three and five return to Hegel's system, not as a set of doctrines, but as a method that sheds light both on scientific models of consciousness and the spiritual dimension of life.

Brains and souls

It is consistent both with Hegel's method and Crick's hypothesis to say that soul is not a substance, not a property, but a process. I go beyond his hypothesis only by expanding the range of its content. Soul is brain/mind engaged in the three kinds of symbolic activity that constitute the spiritual dimension of life, namely aesthetics, religion, and ethics.

The validity of symbols that express the spiritual dimension of life do not depend upon a mind (or soul) separate from the brain. They are events of the undivided mind/brain unity. True neurobiological reduction does not eliminate mental states that manifestly exist. Instead, it eliminates the unreal split between those states and brain events, removing the pseudo-distance between brain and consciousness. As James Ashbrook suggests, neurobiological processes that produce meaning are the soul. He regards the soul as "meaningful memory" of personal, cultural, and religious symbols. It is the core of a person or group and includes a "working memory of personally purposeful behavior." Brain and mind, Ashbrook writes, are "not different" even when we distinguish them: "'Brain' and 'mind' are interchangeable terms. As the subjective experience of objects, the brain is mind; as an objective system external to conscious experience, the mind is brain" (Ashbrook 1989: 75).

True neurobiological reduction maintains the unity of brain and mind without denigrating either aspect of it. I argue that this position is both consistent with scientific evidence and does not undermine the spiritual dimension of life. At the same time, it does not eliminate our tragic awareness of the brain's supreme vulnerability, the threat of meaninglessness and our struggle against it.

Can a machine be conscious?

Chapter 6 returns to Roger Penrose's argument that consciousness is not computable. The fact that we can program computers to perform certain functions even more intelligently than human brains does not mean that they are therefore capable of being conscious. But this does not rule out the possibility that some future machine essentially different from existing computers might be conscious.

Oddly enough, McGinn admits the theoretical possibility of constructing a conscious machine (McGinn 1991: 206–13), even though he thinks it is impossible in principle to explain how the brain becomes conscious. But I argue that science might eventually discover how this occurs and, further, since consciousness is a physical process, that it could be produced in any physical medium adequate to its unique kinds of complexity, either cellular or cybernetic. William Calvin reaches a similar conclusion when he argues that the crucial question about consciousness is *how* it occurs, not where. He speculates that a "Darwin Machine" might be capable of the kind of process that produces consciousness. This would be a computer that "shapes up thoughts in milliseconds rather than millennia, and uses innocuous remembered environments rather than noxious real life ones. It may well create the uniquely human aspect of our consciousness" (Calvin 1990: 262).

Are we determined?

Recent evidence about genetic predisposition to mental conditions like depression underscores the fact that we are significantly determined by our biological nature. The fact that drugs alter mental states with increasing effectiveness also confirms this truth. The claim that we have no autonomy at all, however, like eliminative reductionism is non-science. Belief in total determinism is a philosophical theory. The opposing theory that we have some limited freedom is more reasonable. As has been claimed, "Assume agency or nothing happens." Agency is the power of self, however limited, to cause, to prevent or to change events.

Assume for the sake of argument, however, that autonomy is an illusion. This assumption, whether reasonable or not, would not invalidate my argument that it is meaningful to wrestle with meaninglessness. The subjectivity that belongs to that wrestling remains steadfastly identical to certain neurological processes. The fact that such processes exist in nature and that they are conscious is what matters. What causes them is irrelevant.

Center of narrative gravity

It is also irrelevant to the same argument whether the self exists or is nothing but a bundle of perceptions. The perceiver experiences self as real and perception as a unified process, but both might actually be made up of chunks, as some scientists suggest. Others, however, like Paul D. MacLean (Chapter 4), believe that certain limbic system structures and functions generate a sense of self and reality. Erich Harth (Chapter 5) believes "self-referent brain processes solve the two "binding" problems of the "apparent perceptive and individual unity" and "the perceived unity of the conscious subject" (Harth 1996: 611, 619).

For the present, I hypothetically follow the suggestion that perception is only chunks and the self does not exist. Philosopher Daniel Dennett, for instance, claims that consciousness is actually discontinuous, contrary to our introspective impression of its unity: He argues that the unity of consciousness is a fictional construct. We believe consciousness is unified, not because it actually is, but because the brain edits the multiplicity into a kind of fictional unity: "There is no single, definitive 'stream of consciousness,' because there is no central Headquarters, no Cartesian Theater where 'it all comes together' for the perusal of a Central Meaner" (Dennett 1991: 257). On the contrary, his "Multiple Drafts model" proposes that "all varieties of perception – indeed, all varieties of thought or mental activity – are accomplished in the brain by parallel, multiple processes of interpretation and elaboration of sensory inputs. Information entering the nervous system is under continuous 'editorial revision'" (Dennett 1991: 111). The brain creates the fiction of a single agent as a center of narrative gravity. Dennett notes that

> These strings or streams of narrative issue forth *as if* from a single source – not just in the obvious physical sense of flowing from one mouth, or one pencil or pen, but in a more subtle sense: their effect on

any audience is to encourage them to (try to) posit a ... *center of narrative gravity*.

(Dennett 1991: 418)

Even though this center we call "self" is an abstraction, Dennett recognizes that it is "remarkably robust." This "narrative selfhood" is the product, not the source, of the tales that we think we spin, but which actually "spin us."

Epilogue: keep the fortress

Rhythm and harmony are the "guard house" of the guardians and of the guardian class within each of us, according to the *Republic*. To say this in Dennett's language, the narrative that chiefly spins the guardians is not mainly the words of music. It is chiefly rhythm and harmony that do this. I argue that they are the musical fortress that survives destruction of the Platonic body/soul dualism and of the kind of hope of immortality that it offers.[3]

Are the "myths" that charm Socrates' fear of death a kind of music? Early in the dialogue, Socrates explains why he has composed music in prison: "The same dream used often to come to me in my past life, appearing in different forms at different times, but always saying the same words, 'Socrates, work at music and compose it'" (Plato 1951: 60E). Socrates says that until his trial he thought *philosophy* was that music: "I supposed that the dream was encouraging me to create the music at which I was working already, for I thought that philosophy was the highest music, and my life was spent in philosophy" (Plato 1951: 61E). Religious myth might also be some kind of music. The musical truth of both stands, even if his theoretical arguments lack logical validity and his religious beliefs are unverifiable.

Socrates tells his friends why he had just composed two pieces of music in the literal sense. One was completely new, a hymn to Apollo, and the other was a recasting of the *fables* of Aesop into verse. Executions could not be carried out during the feast of Apollo, and it was delayed longer than expected since contrary winds delayed the ship whose return marked completion of the sacred time: "But then after the trial, when the feast of the god delayed my death ... I composed a hymn to the god whose feast it was." Then Socrates immediately turned Aesop into verse: "I reflected that a man who means to be a poet has to use fiction and not facts for his poems; and I could not invent fiction myself" (Plato 1951: 61D). By recasting these fables into rhythmic verse, Socrates bestows a poetic harmony upon the words that goes beyond what they are in themselves.

Chapter 2

Light and dark[1]

A fact emerges into existence when all the conditions are present, according to G.W.F. Hegel. They come together in such a way that form its ground, which then vanishes by translating itself into the new fact that proceeds from it: "For example," Hegel writes, "the lightning-flash which has set a house on fire would be considered the ground of the conflagration: or the manners of a nation and the condition of its life would be regarded as the ground of its constitution" (Hegel 1892 [1817]: Sec. 123).

It normally takes many conditions to ground a new fact, and initially they might not be related to one another. Each could have its own existence and separate history. At the critical moment, however, they cease to be separate and cause the new fact to come into existence by coalescing. This sometimes happens because a person deliberately makes the conditions come together. Facts can also emerge because the conditions come together on their own apart from deliberate intervention. Biological evolution, politics, and interpersonal relations often seem to follow this model. Such events are not predetermined by the result; the outcome does not dictate the process that leads to it. On the contrary, judgments about their purpose are retrospective. They are *"post-destined."*

The triune brain

Paul D. MacLean, MD (Senior Research Scientist, National Institute of Mental Health), hypothesizes that our forebrains have retained the earlier stages of their evolutionary development. The *reptilian* brain survives in our basal ganglia, while the structures inherited from the "lower mammals" are the *paleomammalian* limbic system. The "late mammalian," or *neomammalian* development is the neocortex of advanced mammals. MacLean represents these structures symbolically (Figure 2) and likens them to three drivers, each with its own mentality, operating an automobile whose brainstem is the chassis. These three forebrain structures are anatomically and chemically different even as they function as a whole. The result is what MacLean calls a "triune" brain, a dialectical

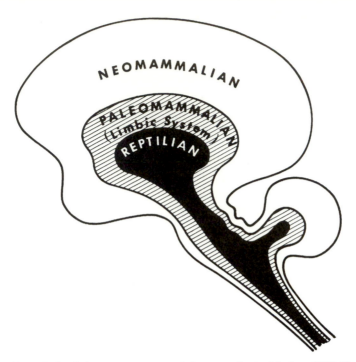

Figure 2 Symbolic representation of the triune brain (Maclean 1990: 9)

interplay of difference and identity. It cannot be reduced simply to "many" or "one" because it is both at the same time. The unity of the three forebrain structures seems to be the center of their narrative history. John Durant attributes the remarkable influence of MacLean's triune brain "metaphor" partly to its simplicity: "MacLean's work represents an island of accessible and wide-ranging generalizations in an ocean of abstruse and arcane technicalities" (Durant 1985: 26).

Pseudo-simplicity

The same "simplicity" might also help explain why MacLean's concept has been misunderstood in a variety of ways. Certain misinterpretations are also premature because critics formulated and hardened them before MacLean completely unfolded his project in a crucial essay (1985) and his most definitive book (1990). One such premature misinterpretation comes from the concept's captivity to the "decade of the beast," which I explain below in my criticism of one of Durant's two major objections.

Durant's other major objection is that MacLean follows the theory that present biological entities recapitulate their evolutionary past. On the contrary, the triune brain concept seems to mean that certain forebrain structures persisted while others changed. As Carl Sagan puts it, the old structures have to keep on working, as in the renovation of a city, while the new ones are being built. This clearly links human brains and behavior with earlier animals, but it does this by focusing on retention, not recapitulation.

MacLean's concept is actually pseudo-simple, because its epic clarity conceals a many-sided complexity. We readily grasp the parts of the triune brain concept one by one, because they are all concrete; but since their meaning is their interconnection, the whole of the concept is not contained in any of its parts. We have to suspend judgment about each of the three structures until we have grasped their unity; yet we cannot grasp their unity without a preview of the parts. That requires looking at each separately as if in a series of one-dimensional still life snapshots of a three-dimensional process, all the while trying to explain how each one fits into a three-dimensional dynamic process. It is excruciatingly difficult to clarify what already looks simple.

Metaphor or hypothesis?

Carl Sagan suggests that the triune brain concept "may prove to be a metaphor of great utility and depth," while Durant claims it is a "very powerful," but misleading, metaphor. The triune brain concept is more than a metaphor; it also contains empirical hypotheses that are verifiable, at least in principle, because they can be tested experimentally. MacLean's basic metaphor seems to be two-sided. One side inspires new empirical hypotheses. The other requires us to interpret the meaning of the experiences it describes. The triune brain concept is less a finished result than a starting point that provokes its students to emerge in new directions. The dynamic nature of concept not only makes it hard to interpret, but there is also a surprising diversity of ways of taking hold of it without misinterpreting it. MacLean is primarily a natural scientist and secondarily a philosopher. However, three philosophical implications of his triune brain concept are especially important.

Solipsism and reality

The philosophy surrounding MacLean's triune brain concept might tend towards solipsism. For instance, he describes space and time as affects, not fixed yardsticks of reality. He writes this about the subjective variations in temporal experience of patients at the beginning of epileptic seizures involving the limbic structures of the temporal lobe:

> As has been described, things seen or heard may give the impression of speeding up or slowing down. A patient may describe the feeling

as though words took a whole minute to be said. Another may experience the feeling of living his life backwards. Things may seem to come to a standstill or, as in delirium, seem to either speed up or slow down.

(MacLean 1990: 450)

Judith Hooper and Dick Teresi quote MacLean's statement about the Big Bang:

But maybe it's an illusion, because it's all being interpreted by the brain, which is just soft mush imprisoned in this bony shell. The brain does everything. It's not your eyes that are looking at me – it's not eyeball to eyeball – it's brain to brain.

(Hooper and Teresi 1986: 46)

This solipsistic tendency stands furthest from my own view than any other part of MacLean's philosophy, but that difference only enhances the dialogue.

Neurobiological reduction

The implicit philosophical principle at the base of the triune brain concept is what I call true neurobiological reduction. MacLean is monistic in holding that there are no mental processes apart from brain events. At the same time, the mental processes have validity, as his criticisms of behaviorism and Bertrand Russell's elimination of subjective states philosophy indicate. His clinical reports cited in Chapter 4 about how patients with limbic epilepsy describe their experiences, and also his own interest in ethology confirm this.

Determinism and autonomy

In 1992 during a private interview, MacLean accepted the term "freedom" as characterizing his triune brain concept and argued that complete determinism is wrong, since the way in which the brain is structured allows seemingly infinite choices. He also said that the brain has graded responses (not merely yes/no), including "almost over the brink." The human brain can make an exceedingly larger number of combinations, although our cultural conditioning limits these choices. Choices are not merely neocortical acts, for sub-neocortical structures of the R-complex and cortical convolution of the limbic system also influence the decisions we make.

MacLean light and dark

MacLean's writings contain both "bright" life-affirming claims about human capabilities and "dark" statements about the malaise of the human predicament. The difference between these two sides of the triune brain concept is partly intrinsic, as I am going to show, and it is also partly historical.

MacLean's first essay in 1949 suggests that limbic paleomammalian processes are irrational and that the frontal lobes might need to override them. These lower processes are

> what we have commonly come to associate with the id, the beast, or sin in man (e.g. gluttony, lechery, etc.). In the light of this it is interesting that through the large uncinate fasciculus, the frontal lobes 'stand guard' over this region. Could it be that feelings of guilt are fomented here?
>
> (MacLean 1949: 347)

MacLean's essay of 1985 and book of 1990 challenge the one-sided, overly pessimistic interpretations of his research that took the 1949 quotation out of context. These more recent works stress the positive contributions that "paleopsychic" processes make to the neocortex. These processes include the "emotional mentation" of the paleomammalian limbic system, the "protomentation" of the reptilian stage, as well as the role of the cerebellum. The link that these primitive brain structures have with the prefrontal lobes, the newest products of brain evolution, produces "rational" behavior. The latest subphase of the evolution of limbic structures makes altruistic behavior possible because the medial dorsal nucleus links them to the prefrontal lobes.

Negative and positive emotions

Ruth Macklin recognized both the dark and light sides of the triune brain concept even before MacLean unfolded his entire project in 1985 (Macklin 1978). She argues that his triune brain can account for both negative and positive emotions.

Negative emotions are irrational in the sense that they lead to destructive behavior. They come from the miserable internal state MacLean calls "schizophysiology," namely the cutting of evolutionarily earlier structures from relation to the neocortical processes that might otherwise override them. Arthur Koestler follows that this 1949 type suggestion is at the "darkest" end of the spectrum of the triune brain concept's interpreters. He claims that man is a freak of nature, miserable because his brain is a mistake of evolution (Koestler 1967).

Positive emotions are rational in the sense that they lead to beneficial behavior and come from a state of internal happiness. MacLean refers to such life-affirming condition in a number of texts, especially since 1985. This example, however, dates from 1962:

> A concern for the welfare of the species is based on sexuality. In the complex organization of old and new structures under consideration, we presumably have a neural ladder, a visionary ladder, for ascending from the most primitive sexual feeling to the highest level of altruistic sentiments.
>
> (MacLean 1962: 299–300)

Both sides exist

Some interpretations of MacLean's hypothesis are pessimistic fixations on the misery of the human species. Others are "life-affirming" and focus on the fact that human beings are capable of altruism and other ennobling mental qualities. I asked MacLean how he viewed these conflicting interpretations of his triune brain hypothesis and the fact that both seem to be based on different sides of it. He answered "I hope both sides exist."

Decade of the beast

The triune brain concept nevertheless gained favor and created resistance during a time of peculiar fixation on the belief that the "beast within" human beings is the source of their destructiveness.

"Crocodile theories," as I call them, grabbed hold of the dark side of MacLean's thinking and begot a grim mystique of how our earlier evolutionary heritage affects us. During the 1970s and a few years immediately before them, as at other times in history, there was a widespread fear that something archaic in our brains might burst through neocortical restraints and jump out of us at any moment. Hooper and Teresi characterize this as the belief that "a primitive reptilian brain lurks in the deepest layers of human neural tissue like a Minotaur in a cave . . . bestial ghosts of our evolutionary past that could actually rear up on their furry or scally hind legs to haunt us" (Hooper and Teresi 1986: 181–2).

Vernon Mark and Frank Ervin attribute the bestial violence in us to the "limbic system," but used the term to include certain structures of the brain stem (mid brain) and what MacLean calls reptilian structures (basal ganglia):

> To sum up: when we refer to the "emotional brain," the "limbic brain," or the "limbic system," we shall mean the cingulum, the hippocampus, the thalamic and hypothalamic nuclei, and the more

complex masses of the basal ganglia, mid brain, and amygdala. This system has a wide range of functions including the modulation and control of fight-or-flight behavior.

(Mark and Ervin 1970: 24)

Crocodile Man, a book by Andre Mayer and Michael Wheeler (1982), reports how this neurological model of human violence was instrumental in the acquittal of a man who tried to murder two girls. During the 1970s, some likened the human condition to riding a wild animal, and others wanted to drug the beast within us.

Durant suggests that "beast in man" themes like these come from the mistaken belief that our nature is a two-fold split into "good and bad, rational and irrational, the controller and the controlled." As a result, "*Homo Sapiens* is two beings in one, beast and part man, and his destiny hangs on the outcome of the continual battle which they wage for the mastery of his life" (Durant 1981: 21–2). This division of human nature into two beings ultimately "goes back in Western culture to the doctrine of original sin" (Durant 1992: 269). Chapter 10 shows that splitting human nature into good and evil parts is actually pre-biblical.

Deconstructing the beast mystique

The beast within man theme that Durant so clearly identifies and rightly criticizes might even be worse than he thinks. What does it say about the human view of other species? Might the decade of the beast have damaged us in ways that Durant does not mention?

War and hunting

Could human destructiveness be a uniquely human type of behavior? Is it possible that our brains became capable of this behavior during a specifically human phase of evolution? The human brain evolved into its present structure long before agricultural life, according to S.L. Washburn and C.S. Lancaster:

> Even 6,000 years ago large parts of the world's population were non-agricultural, and the entire evolution of man from the earliest populations of *Homo erectus* to the existing races took place during the period in which man was a hunter. The common factors that dominated human evolution and produced *Homo sapiens* were preagricultural. Agricultural ways of life have dominated less than 1 percent of human history, and there is no evidence of major biological changes during that period of time.
>
> (Washburn and Lancaster 1993: 213)

Some consider it naive to criticize hunting animals. At the same time no type of behavior ought to be self-certifying in such a way that it cannot be questioned. Washburn and Lancaster suggest that hunting disrupted man's unity with other animals and changed his "view of what is natural." It made him think that "it is normal for animals to flee" because they are wild:

> Prior to hunting, the relations of our ancestors to other animals must have been very much like those of the other noncarnivores. They could have moved close among the other species, fed beside them, and shared the same waterholes. But with the origin of human hunting, the peaceful relationship was destroyed, and for at least half a million years man has been the enemy of even the largest mammals. In this way the whole human view of what is normal and natural in the relation of man to animals is a product of hunting, and the world of flight and fear is the result of the efficiency of the hunters.
>
> (Washburn and Lancaster 1993: 216)

Book II of Plato's *Republic* speculates about a possible connection between eating meat and the kind of greed that leads to war. Socrates says this:

> Then must we cut off a piece of our neighbors' land, if we are going to have sufficient for pasture and tillage, and they in turn from ours, if they let themselves go to the unlimited acquisition of money, overstepping the boundary of the necessary?
>
> (Plato 1968: 373D)

Winning tribal battles had survival value at the same time as hunting animals did. War was once "viewed in much the same way as hunting," according to Washburn and Lancaster:

> Other human beings were simply the most dangerous game. War has been far too important in human history for it to be other than pleasurable for the males involved. It is only recently, with the entire change in the nature and conditions of war, that this institution has been challenged, that the wisdom of war as a normal part of national policy or as an approved road to personal social glory has been questioned.
>
> (Washburn and Lancaster 1993: 216)

Human beings seem to lack certain biological controls over killing their own species, and this is what separates human behavior "from that of other carnivorous mammals." This may be one reason why the human species is more violent than others. There is more than one way of interpreting why this is the case:

> It may be that human hunting is so recent from an evolutionary point of view that there was not enough time for controls to evolve. Or it may be that killing other human beings was a part of the adaptation from the beginning, and our sharp separation of war from hunting is due to the recent development of these institutions. Or it may be simply that in most human behavior stimulus and response are not tightly bound.
>
> (Washburn and Lancaster 1993: 216–17)

In any case, it is tragically clear that most human societies have permitted, often encouraged, killing human beings from societies other than their own. This might shed light on the connection between violence and power worship.

Slow hook "sport"

According to Washburn and Lancaster, hunting established a world view and certain ways of acting that still persist because evolution might have built "a relation between biology, psychology, and behavior." This might explain certain patterns of behavior that are "both easily learned and pleasurable." The enjoyment some find in hunting, even though it is no longer economically necessary, is one such pattern of behavior. "Part of the motivation for hunting is the immediate pleasure it gives the hunter" and "the extent of the efforts devoted to maintain killing as a sport." It is distasteful to think that human beings enjoy destroying living things, but Washburn and Lancaster point out that "we all know people who use the lightest fishing tackle to prolong the fish's futile struggle, in order to maximize the personal sense of mastery and skill" (Washburn and Lancaster 1993: 216). I call this *slow hook "sport,"* a genuinely tragic way to kill something.

Which beast leapt out?

Why do school yard bullies and other tyrants consider their cruelty "sport"? Does the suggestion that war is human hunting shed any light on human behavior? Is it possible that *blaming* the beast within us for our violence might spring from some distorted reminiscent awareness that we became violent through *hunting* beasts? Something terrible did leap out during the decade of the beast, but it seems to be entirely human.

In 1974 I noticed a qualitative leap into a new kind of cultural degradation which I criticize in Chapter 7. Verbal violence had gradually built up to the point that it seemed to cross a node then, and it was clear that a new epoch of cynical egotism had emerged, at least in the US. Deterioration seemed more subtle in the UK, as I compared changes I had perceived during visits to Britain over the previous 15 years. The change there seemed too nebulous to capture, but it clarified my perspective on what had happened in the US. As a result, an outline of the phenomenology of four types of everyday language of degradation dictated itself to me on the train between Cambridge and London:

> *Needling* is the kind of verbal torture that indirectly expresses cruelty.
>
> *Reality Distortion* is deception about facts ... it warps thought and perception by implanting irrational mental processes in the Victim.
>
> *Debunking* is deception about values. It is the use of fallacious language to foul those qualities that are life-giving ... by turning the good into a sickened version of itself.
>
> *Levelling*, the social dimension in which the three other types operate, is the collective ... lowering of anything interesting to a state of unimportance.
>
> (Keyes 1989: 2–3)

The beast that leapt out with all of this was not a hold-over from some other species. It was the all too human ego at its worst, hunting victims, "sporting" with them, and tyranically relativizing them:

> Power hungry egotism relativizes the other and treats it, him, or her, as a property of the self. *Such egotism is the illusion of entitlement to the right to treat the other as a tool that serves the interest of being-for-self.*
>
> (Keyes 1989: 14)

Were various kinds of degrading language among the conditions that coalesced to form the ground from which power hungry egotism emerged? Or did other conditions not identified here come together to produce it? Or could all of these facts have emerged more or less independently of one another? Is it possible for all of them to be the conditions that will force *something else* to come into existence?

One thing seems to be clear, namely that no person or specific group of persons intentionally caused these facts to emerge in the decade of the beast. The whole syndrome seems to have been postdestined. At the same time, it and syndromes like it operate as if they had a mind of their own. My report on degrading language attributes something like an anonymous mind to the "prejudices of the times" that seem to have a collective existence apart from the individuals who participate in them. How can we explain the fact that large numbers of people suddenly start thinking, acting, and feeling similarly? MacLean's discussion of "isopraxic" behavior (Chapter 3) might be relevant to the question.

Sagan and Durant on Plato's *Phaedrus*

The fact that some mistook which beast is to be feared and read MacLean's concept through the lenses of that mistake does not invalidate the true meaning of his concept. The clue is clarifying *which* Platonic beast scheme applies to MacLean's concept.

Sagan thinks MacLean's triune brain concept is remarkably similar to Plato's image of the soul as a charioteer and two horses in the *Phaedrus* (Sagan 1977: 82–3). He refers to the well-known Platonic metaphor of the soul:

> Let it be likened to the union of powers in a team of winged steeds and their winged charioteer. Now all the gods' steeds and all their charioteers are good, and of good stock; but with other beings it is not wholly so. With us men, in the first place, it is a pair of steeds that the charioteer controls; moreover one of them is noble and good, and of good stock, while the other has the opposite character, and his stock is opposite. Hence the task of our charioteer is difficult and troublesome.
>
> (Plato 1972: 246A–B)

Sagan interprets Plato's driver as MacLean's late mammalian brain and the two horses as the two more primitive brains.

MacLean does not attribute as much sovereignty to the late mammalian brain as Sagan does. Nor are his two older drivers always in conflict with one another. MacLean's reptilian part is not always violent, as Sagan's comment implies: "Deep inside the skull of everyone there is something like the brain of a crocodile" (Sagan 1980: 276–7). There is also evidence that some ways in which crocodiles treat their offspring are beneficent, and reptiles often stop short of killing their own kind during conflict. We would have to change the *Phaedrus* model to make it fit the triune brain concept. That means replacing the lone driver inside the chariot with the three drivers trying to control conflict.

Sagan's *Phaedrus* comparison nevertheless controls Durant's view of MacLean's concept: the lone driver inside the chariot is the human part, while the two horses together are the bestial part. Durant uses this interpretation to confirm his main criticism: MacLean's concept divides human nature into the two beings that go back to the idea of original sin. Durant thinks that this "metaphor" invites turning the bestial part into the beast within us that threatens to break lose and do harm. The beasts

MacLean finds in us, however, are beneficial as well as harmful, both light and dark. The main problem with Durant's criticism, as well as of Sagan's use of the *Phaedrus* model, is that MacLean's three-in-one does not reduce to a two-in-one.

Plato's many-headed, many-colored beast

Plato divides the soul into three parts: one that desires, another that is spirited (aggressive), and still another that learns. These respectively love gain, honor, and wisdom. He has Socrates invite us "to see" what we ourselves look like as a triune combination in beast terms in Book 9 of the *Republic*:

> "Well, then, mold a single *idea* for a many-colored, many-headed beast that has a ring of heads of tame and savage beasts and can change them and make all of them grow from itself."

> "That's a job for a clever molder," he said. "But, nevertheless, since speech is more easily molded than wax and the like, consider it as molded."

> "Now, then, mold another single *idea* for a lion, and a single one for a human being. Let the first be by far the greatest, and the second, second in size."

> "That's easier," he said, "and the molding is done."

> "Well, then, join them – they are three – in one, so that in some way they grow naturally together with each other."

> "They are joined," he said.

> "Then mold about them on the outside an image of one – that of the human being – so that to the man who's not able to see what's inside, but sees only the outer shell, it looks like one animal, a human being."

> (Plato 1968: 588C–E)

Plato light and dark

The beasts within us are miserable (unjust) when they lack harmony and conflict with one another. This happens when reason loses control of the whole because we

> make strong the manifold beast and the lion and what's connected with the lion, while starving the human being and making him so weak that he can be drawn wherever either of the others leads and

doesn't habituate them to one another or make them friends but lets them bite and fight and devour each other.

(Plato 1968: 588E–589A)

All the same beasts within us are happy (just) when they are in harmony. Reason produces the harmony when it takes

charge of the many-headed beast – like a farmer, nourishing and cultivating the tame heads, while hindering the growth of the savage ones – making the lion's nature an ally and, caring for all in common, making them friends with each other and himself, and so rear them.

(Plato 1968: 589B)

Two kinds of taste

The two horses of the *Phaedrus* stand for the conflicting tastes and corresponding ways of existing that lead to justice and injustice. They and the charioteer are not parts of the soul's structure. They are operational "parts," depictions of different ways of behaving, similar to Macklin's rational and irrational emotions. The good horse seeks the kind of knowledge that leads to reason's harmony, while the other neglects it on account of its gluttony for the food of opinion:

Now of the steeds, so we declare, one is good and the other is not; but we have not described the excellence of the one nor the badness of the other, and that is what must now be done. He that is on the more honourable side is upright and clean-limbed, carrying his neck high, with something of a hooked nose: in colour he is white, with black eyes: a lover of glory, but with temperance and modesty: one that consorts with genuine renown, and needs no whip, being driven by the word of command alone. The other is crooked of frame, a massive jumble of a creature, with thick short neck, snub nose, black skin, and grey eyes; hot-blooded, consorting with wantonness and vainglory; shaggy of ear, deaf, and hard to control with whip and goad.

(Plato 1972: 253C–D)

Well-mannered lizards

The three-fold Platonic scheme and the three forebrain structures of MacLean's concept are both "triune." There are also other important similarities. The tame and savage beasts partly resemble the protoreptilian brain, as the lion does the paleomammalian, and as the human head is neomammalian. Even though the content of the two models differs in certain respects, the beasts of both models are neither treacherous nor beneficent in themselves. In both models, whether the beasts cause happiness or misery depends on the presence or absence of harmony.

MacLean's beasts, like Plato's, are both tame and wild, and certain wild ones are tamable. Our more primitive brain structures are both destructive and beneficial, dark and light. There are also shadow mixtures, as well as combinations of them that cannot be reduced to story book caricatures. We have to correct Sagan's thoughtful crocodile comment to read that the brain of each of us contains "something like a crocodile and a well-mannered lizard, too."

Epilogue: brains and souls

MacLean deconstructs the Platonic split between body and soul by recasting the beast metaphor in the *Republic* in biological terms, thereby attributing to the brain/mind unity some of the qualities Plato thinks belong to the soul. Not only is MacLean's triune brain concept a monistic restatement of the main outlines of Plato's three structures of the soul, but it also recasts the just and unjust ways in which they function in relation to one another. This suggests that "soul" is more than certain mental states like those mentioned in the preceding chapter.

At an even more basic level, soul is a "self-instantiating" process, according to Brian Cooney. He thinks that MacLean presupposes something like an Aristotelian and functionalist view of the soul. Cooney defines self-instantiation as the means by which any kind of system "responds to environmental events in such a way as to secure its capacity to respond to the same kinds of events in the same ways" (Cooney 1991: 220).

Biological entities maintain themselves over time through "self-instantiating information," according to Cooney. This information "modulates" the "response-selecting component" of their control systems, and an individual person's ability to do this depends on higher level neural information which cannot be reduced to its lower level constituents. Self-instantiating information is "distinct from its physical embodiment at any point in the organism's duration, even though it cannot exist without embodiment in the appropriate *kind* of physical system" (Cooney 1992: 2). At the same time, it does not emerge from the brain, as a variety of "property dualists" claim, but remains integral to the brain/mind unity throughout the entire process. Cooney has Daniel Dennett's center of narrative gravity in mind when he refers to the narrative effect of self-instantiation: "Human personal existence has a narrative structure, a beginning, middle, and end, 'not merely' a repetitive acting out of instinctive repertoires" (Cooney 1992: 2).

Part two

Beasts within [1]

Beasts as such are ethically innocent. Reptilian behavior is life-affirming in reptiles since it is the way in which they survive and adapt to one another and their environment. By contrast human beasts are simultaneously innocent and guilty. Limbic emotion and neocortical calculation make reptilian behavior tragically ambivalent when it is extrapolated into human terms. In us it is both a danger to life and *also* life-affirming, both a crocodile and a well-mannered lizard.

Chapter 3 shows that Paul D. MacLean sees both sides of the reptilian beasts within us, in spite of misinterpretations of his hypothesis by others. Territoriality, hierarchies, ritual, and other primal reptilian traits in human beings are both light and dark. Chapter 4 traces conviction, the feeling that something is ultimately important, to our paleomammalian limbic brains. This too has light and dark sides since conviction does not guarantee truth. In itself it does not know how to distinguish between scientific knowledge and superstition. The neocortex has to teach it the difference.

The limbic brain attaches affective importance upon everything reptiles do, and this intensifies the human bestial ambivalence of beneficent and destructive behavior. Limbic feelings, moreover, are both hostile and loving in themselves. The latest subphase of limbic evolution adds the neurobiologic capability of a new kind of familial love: nursing, audio-vocal contact, and play. Just as the human neocortex must stand guard over limbic conviction, our limbic bestial brains inspire the neocortex to be ethical. MacLean presents evidence that the human pre-frontal lobes are linked to the limbic system in such a way that we can generalize the paleomammalian responsibility for nursing offspring into ethical concern for life, human and otherwise. He calls this *conscience*.

> What is substantially new in the known history of biology is that this concern extends not only to the human family, but to all living things – an evolutionary turnabout that could affect a turnabout in what has heretofore seemed a vicious life – death struggle long recognized as the struggle between good and evil.
>
> (MacLean 1990: 562)

This means that the neurobiological roots of beneficence, as well as destructiveness, are pre-neocortical. The biological origins of ethics are earlier than the human species, if MacLean is right; but we could also use the same hypothesis to help clarify the evolutionary origins of aesthetics as well as ethics. Reptilian behavioral sequences are a kind of non-auditory primal musical rhythm and harmony, while play and a wide range of limbic feelings, including conviction, are essential to human musical expression.

Chapter 3

Crocodiles and well-mannered lizards

When the Callixylon Tree was alive about 250 million years ago, all the earth was one giant continent, which we call Pangaea. Mammal-like reptiles called therapsids (Figure 3) inhabited the earth then, and their skeletons have been found in every continent. These advanced reptiles are close to human evolutionary origins, since they were the source of all subsequent mammals. MacLean points out that the flesh-eating types look somewhat like wolves and dogs: "Unlike their waddling predecessors, these animals had become upright and, with legs supporting them from underneath, were able to run swiftly. The jaws and teeth, and other cranial features, were approaching the mammalian condition" (MacLean 1985: 408).

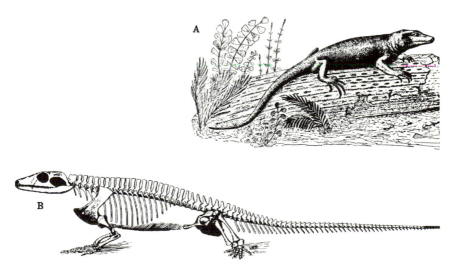

Figure 3 Therapsids: Williston's (1925) conception of the lizardlike appearance of *Varanosaurus*, a primitive mammal-like reptile (A), based on his reconstruction of the skeleton shown beneath (B) (MacLean 1990: 101)

The ancestry of the "R-complex" ("striatal complex") of the human brain goes back to these creatures, according to MacLean. Its seat is the basal ganglia, the phylogenetically oldest part of the forebrain. These ganglia make up about three-quarters of its gray matter of the forebrain and include the olfactostriatum, corpus striatum (caudate nucleus and putamen), and globus pallidus (or pallidum).

No reptiles that exist today are directly in line with these distant ancestors of mammals, which means that we cannot directly reconstruct their mentality. As a result, MacLean constructs a model of the mentality of the reptilian brain by studying lizards. His characterization of the reptilian mentality also seems to describe much that human beings and other mammals do.

Instinct alone does not explain what reptiles do, and their behavior shows that they also have considerable "capacity for experiential learning and memory" (MacLean 1990: 150). While lizards are thought to be poor learners, some researchers have found that "if given the opportunity to work for the reward of heat from a lamp, they may show themselves to be remarkably apt learners" (MacLean 1990: 149). Learning is essentially beneficial because it expands the range of possibilities for survival. Whether it is actually beneficial, however, depends on what is learned. Truth is beneficial; sophistic deception is harmful.

Domain and territoriality

An organism's territory is the operational space needed "for both self-preservation and the preservation of the species." These activities require a homesite, a space the animal defends, and a home range, a space the animal uses but does not defend. The life-preserving activities of an animal's domain (e.g., "a place to hunt for food, and a place to mate and to breed") require a protected area.

Territoriality is an animal's "demonstrated determination to protect a particular piece of ground" (MacLean 1990: 229). For some animals, this area is a fixed territory. Migratory animals, however, have "moving territories," which are more like a "social" or "conceptual" space that strange animals are not allowed to enter (MacLean 1990: 230).

Marking and patrolling territories

Cats and dogs mark their territory by urinating on their boundaries. Other animals use optical rather than olfactory means. Hence some monkeys "sit at lookout sites with their thighs spread and a display of partial erection while the rest of the animals feed or take a siesta" (MacLean 1990: 231). Human counterparts can possibly be seen in mythological representations of "Pan, Priapus, Amon, Min, and others" who are "often portrayed with an enlarged or erect phallus that is superstitiously endowed with the power of protection" (MacLean 1990: 231).

Human beings have also used phallic symbolism, including "stone monuments showing an erect phallus," to protect their territories. MacLean suggests that human beings might even use territorial markers of a subtler nature: "Vandalism and graffiti would seem to be a form of visual marking. A refined type of visual marking is typified by signing a guest book upon ceremonial occasions" (MacLean 1990: 231). Furthermore, human beings also seem to mark and protect "conceptual spaces." These include boundaries such as countries, institutions, businesses, and even outer space. MacLean notes that "Many teachers and scientists have the reputation of establishing intellectual and research territories and protecting them with all their might" (MacLean 1990: 231).

Animals also patrol their territories, of course. This is the case with black lizards, far-ranging wolves, and wild chimpanzees that roam and challenge intruders in silence: "Among human beings regular patrolling of territory is best illustrated by military groups" (MacLean 1990: 232).

Territorial potential

Animals do not demonstrate the determination to defend a fixed territory if they are migratory or if they live in such low density that "not even their home ranges overlap" (MacLean 1990: 103). But this does not mean, as is sometimes supposed, that such animals lack a territorial potential. If circumstances such as food supply force the same lizards to start living in high density, their territoriality can take the shape of hostility to one another: "If two neighbors found themselves too close, both would show a threatening attitude, raising themselves on stiff legs and strutting up and down with their dorsal combs elevated" (MacLean 1990: 138). Instead of showing antagonism to one another, they sometimes become collectively passive: "These sleek, sand-colored animals lay straddling one another in a languid state, somewhat as one would imagine Milton's stunned and fallen angels after their crash from paradise" (MacLean 1990: 139).

Hierarchies

The same lizards that did not seem to be hierarchical when they are widely dispersed become so in high density. They developed a social hierarchy dominated by one "tyrant" male lizard that "regularly threatened the others and preempted the right to temporarily trespass on their resting areas." The tyrant will sometimes harass a subordinate male that cannot escape, even tormenting him (MacLean 1990: 139–40). However, by yielding to the tyrant, the other lizards gained the security of a dwelling place on the rock wall as well as abundant food (MacLean 1990: 105).

Nativism

These "lesser" lizards became nativistic and defended the same tyrant that dominates them if an alien male lizard intrudes into their territory. MacLean cites additional animal examples of nativism:

> In regard to nativistic responses, it is also of comparative interest that if one removes a turkey, say, from a confined flock, or indeed takes a young dog from its littermates in an enclosure, it will be attacked as if a stranger when reintroduced to the group (even after a period as short as five minutes).
>
> (MacLean 1990: 567)

Strangeness

The ability to recognize strangeness and familiarity are "opposite sides of the same coin," since the ability to recognize what is strange "depends on a contrast with what is familiar." Communal groups of lizards "gang-up" against newcomers to defend their territory, partly because of their innate ability to recognize strangeness.

The reptilian reaction to strangeness can express itself as intolerance of blemishes. This drive to harass blemished individuals extends beyond reptiles:

> It is a familiar observation among those who are pigeon fanciers or who raise poultry that a fowl with an open injury may be relentlessly pecked to death by members of the flock, an observation illustrating that blemishes also precipitate group harassment.
>
> (MacLean 1990: 568)

MacLean pointed out in a private interview that human beings seem to tolerate handicaps that could be construed as blemishes more than other species. This suggests a tendency to control the reptilian drive, with the result that human beings are ambivalent about blemishes. On the other hand, many human beings harass individuals with "blemishes," regardless of whether these are physical, behavioral, or "differences in religious or political views" (MacLean 1996: 568).

Routinizing behavior

Lizards have two types of daily routines. First, the master routines a lizard follows structure its day as a whole. For instance, in certain types of lizards a slow, cautious emergence in the morning precedes a preliminary period of basking; this is followed by defecation, local foraging, and an inactive period, which in turn are followed by foraging farther afield, return to the shelter area, and retirement to a shelter or roost. Second, subroutines, which are equally structured, "apply to habitual and individually typical acts that are carried out during the course of the master routine" (MacLean 1990: 142).

"Routinizing behavior" is the "*round-the-clock*, temporal sequencing of behavior," the regulation of the *order* and *time* in which daily routines occur. *Rituals* are subroutines that have "become rigidly structured in their patterns and time of occurrence" (MacLean 1990: 143). *Precedent* is the habitual following of a subroutine that initially occurred and through "some fortuitous circumstance" had survival value (MacLean 1990: 143).

The human need for routine, precedent, and ritual seems to arise from reptilian drives like those mentioned above. MacLean gives a variety of examples about how routine dissipates human anxiety, one of which is a study of the great concern on the part of school children to follow a single route to school for fear of the consequences of changing their path (MacLean 1990: 237). He also mentions the search for legal precedent and academic routines. "The stress generated by an actual or threatened change in routine is many times compounded when entire organizations are involved, as exemplified at the institutional level by the upheaval resulting from proposed drastic alterations in the curriculum at a school or university" (MacLean 1990: 238).

Isopraxic and tropistic behavior

Isopraxic behavior consists in "performing or acting in a like manner," "doing something the same way," "behaving in the same way." The unfamiliar word is used to avoid causal explanations of "species-typical" behavior in which "animals engage simultaneously in the same kind of species-typical activity" (MacLean 1990: 143). By calling this kind of behavior "isopraxic," we suspend judgment about whether or not it occurs naturally or is learned. Human imitative behavior "may have some protective value by signifying, 'I am like you'" (MacLean 1990: 239). Could this help explain how the "prejudices of the times" (noted in the preceding chapter) are like an "anonymous mind" that seems to operate collectively "apart from the individuals who participate in them"?

Tropism is an unexplained "positive or negative response of an animal to partial or complete representations, whether alive or inanimate" (MacLean 1990: 145). MacLean distinguishes two basic kinds of tropistic behavior. First, "imprinting," which MacLean characterizes as an innate tendency to learn, can be found in some birds, but not in lizards. It is "the situation in which a young bird during a critical period attaches itself to the first creature it meets" (MacLean 1990: 146). Second, "fixed action patterns" are an innate response to certain stimuli, such as form, movement, or color. For instance, certain fish respond by fighting when they see the color red even on the belly of a dummy (MacLean 1990: 145). Some fixed action patterns, however, are elicited by partial representations. Instances of this include "a rooster that regularly mated with a feather on the ground," a hog that ejaculated upon encountering the "hide of a sow on a wooden dummy," and human sexual fetishes (MacLean 1990: 239).

Tropistic tendencies in human beings might partly explain their responses to Rorschach inkblot tests as well as to "visual and performing arts, commercial advertising, and various other sources." For instance, MacLean cites arguments that "cubistic painting owes some of its appeal to the portrayal of archetypal patterns and partial representations, such as, for example, a Picasso painting showing the human figure in two dimensions, with the eyes and buttocks in the same plane" (MacLean 1990: 240).

The neural mechanisms that make this type of behavior possible in species with higher brain structures might be based upon the "selective responses" of individual cells and the sensory networks to which they belong. In the visual system, for instance, specific cells have been reported to respond "to specific aspects of stimulus objects such as edges, contrast, orientation, directional movement, color, and so forth." There is also evidence that the auditory systems of squirrel monkeys contain some cells responsive only to the species-typical vocalizations of another squirrel monkey. MacLean speculates that certain partial representations might activate the cells within neural networks "genetically tuned" to such partial representations (MacLean 1990: 240).

Repetitious behavior

Performing a specific act over and over again is "repetitious behavior." It reinforces and assures communication of signals. Examples include: signature and challenge courtship displays by lizards, some human courtship activities such as frequent telephone calls, and Lady Macbeth's compulsive hand washing. Displacement behavior is a type of repetitiousness that seems "inappropriate for a particular occasion." Instances of this include "the disproportionate increase of tongue flicks observed when increasing numbers of Komodo monitors meet at carrion," or "a bird's preening in a threatening situation" (MacLean 1990: 147, 241), and certain types of mammalian behavior. MacLean speculates that in mammals such behavior involves the limbic system, as well as the striatal complex. Mammals might engage in displacement behavior as a way of trying to restore or repair function in the presence of stress:

Human "displacement" reactions during uneasy moments may

become more manageable when they are recognized for what they are – e.g., grooming and cleaning reactions such as scratching the head, rubbing the face or hands, clearing the throat, picking the nose, biting nails, spitting, and so forth. A well-known conductor remarked that on the day of a concert, "I insist on being scrupulously clean. Even if I have had two showers already, ... I take another. It's a ritualistic approach." At the institutional level displacement propensities may take the form of such time-honored procedures as appointing an ad hoc committee. It seems to be understood in universities, as well as in government, that at any one time the number of existing committees is a measure of existing tension.

(MacLean 1990: 241)

Reenactment behavior

This form of behavior is "a repeated performance in which a number of actions are meaningfully related." Reenactment subroutines are always based on a precedent. It differs from an animal's reenactment of its daily master routine, such as the lizard's "emerging, basking, defecating, and so forth." Reptilian examples of reenactment behavior include the "retirement-to-shelter" behavior of rainbow lizards, the nesting behavior of sea-turtles, and egg-laying reenactment of iguana lizards (MacLean 1990: 147–8, 242).

Precedent also explains certain types of human behavior, for instance birthdays and national holidays. Furthermore, reenactment subroutines may have either a superstitious or more rational origin. Groundhog Day was probably based on superstition; however, the customs of cooking corn with salt and the ban against eating uncooked pork "appear to have insinuated their way into the collective human consciousness through a cerebral learning process quite unlike that of Pavlovian conditioning, and perhaps more akin to what induces 'bait shyness'" (MacLean 1990: 242). Other examples of human reenactment behavior include ritualized subroutines that occur either on a single day or periodically, e.g., weekly church attendance, yearly graduation exercises. The fact that reenactment behavior signifies a number of meaningfully related acts distinguishes it from repetitiousness. Just as Lady Macbeth's hand washing is repetitious if viewed as a specific act, it is an instance of reenactment behavior if we see it in the context of the entire scene (MacLean 1990: 147).

Deceptive behavior

This form of behavior is one of the most essential for the survival of reptiles. They use it not only to obtain the "necessities of life (e.g., a home base, food, mate)" but also to avoid "virtual elimination or death through the actions of others . . . it requires more guise and ruse to avoid failure than to achieve success" (MacLean 1990: 148).

The natural markings of certain species are sometimes deceptive apart from behavior. The term "automimicry" refers to superficial resemblances between parts of the same animal. One illustration of this is found in the type of snake that has a "marking on the tip of its tail that mimics the eye in the head" (MacLean 1990: 149). Other interesting illustrations can be found in the "markings on the head that make the size of the horns of a stag or ram seem larger; colorations that enhance the size of the eye; hair tufts or white streaks on the side of the cheek that amplify the size of the canines." MacLean also cites Morris who "suggests that the breasts of women represent a form of automimicry, giving in face-on meetings the appearance of buttocks" (MacLean 1990: 235).

Some deception is more explicitly behavioral. MacLean describes female lizards that sometimes "perform enticement displays as though inviting courtship and mating by a male, but will then run away or fight the male off if he takes hold of her" (MacLean 1990: 148). Reptilian stalking of prey sometimes includes deceptive behavior, as, for instance, in the way Komodo lizards stalk deer for days at a time or wait in ambush for hours (MacLean 1990: 242).

Human deceptiveness sometimes resembles reptilian behavior. MacLean writes that certain recent assassins of Presidents have stalked their prey in a way similar to the Komodo dragon. Deception can be found in the highest echelons of government, as the indictment suggests: "the conspirators would by deceit, craft, trickery, and dishonest means defraud . . . . The conspirators would give false, misleading, evasive and deceptive statements and testimony." MacLean asks some questions about why human beings take risk so much in order to deceive: "Why do the games that we teach our young place such a premium on deceptive tactics and terminology of deception? How can pupils be expected to come off the playing field and not use the same principles in competition and struggle for survival in the classroom?" (MacLean 1990: 242).

Deceptive behavior is one of the most serious ethical problems that arises from protomentation. The criticism of sophistical deception in the *Republic* illustrates its relation to the misuse of power:

> For, as to getting away with it, we'll organize secret societies and clubs; and there are teachers of persuasion who offer the wisdom of the public assembly and the court. On this basis, in some things we'll persuade and in others use force; thus we'll get the better and not pay the penalty.
>
> (Plato 1968: 365D)

Truth ought to triumph over reptilian deception. However, one could ask whether deception is ever ethically justified. For instance, is it wrong to lie to prevent murder? Is it wrong, as the ancient Chinese text by Sun Tzu (1971) suggests, to deceive the enemy general in war in order to prevent killing troops and destroying cities?

Non-verbal communication

Survival depends partly upon non-verbal communication, "prosematic behavior," as MacLean calls it. Lizards communicate with one another by displays to differentiate between sexes, to recognize and communicate with other members of the same species, etc. Four such displays have been identified.

"Signature" display

A signature display, consisting perhaps of a single pushup followed by two head bobs, means something like "Take notice." It is also used socially as: a greeting between two or more lizards, the male's initiation of courtship, and the male's first reaction when he encounters another lizard intruding into his territory. This "assertive" type of behavior can also occur in non-social situations, e.g. "after a lizard moves to a new perch" even when no other lizards are present.

Territorial challenge

Territorial display is the tenant lizard's challenge if an intruder ignores his initial signature display. This challenge display begins with a single push-up followed by a number of head bobs. This is accompanied by extension of the throat fold and a narrowing of the defender's body that exposes his coloration. If this is not effective, the defender will run towards the intruder "in a loping gait" and then "turn the body sideways somewhat in the manner of a football player attempting to block." If necessary, the defender will "face-off" the intruder and fight him, risking even loss of his tail, until one of them bows in submission (MacLean 1990: 109).

The behavior of some mammals is strikingly similar to "the 'close-in' challenge display of territorial lizards." MacLean cites instances of these similarities in the sideways presentations of rodents and monkeys. The Komodo dragon's goose-stepping gait and the "stilted, staccato steps of the displays of the great apes" suggest human similarities. MacLean says that this kind of gait and the sideways presentation "have such an uncanny resemblance that it would almost seem that the challenge display has been genetically packaged and handed up the phylogenetic tree of mammals" (MacLean 1990: 233).

Symbolic equivalents

Mammals sometimes use sex organs or their "symbolic equivalents" to express reptilian-based instincts, such as challenge displays, according to MacLean. For instance, certain Melanesian rituals are similar to the reptilian-type challenge displays of squirrel monkeys: "When frightened, excited, elated, or surprised, . . . men and boys spontaneously meet the precipitating event by a penile display dance" (MacLean 1990: 233).

Eyes sometimes seem to become equivalent to sex organs in challenge displays: "It was as though the eye and the genital acquire an equivalent meaning through generalization." Organs such as the tongue and the hands, which can be used to signify the sex act, are also sometimes used to threaten. MacLean explains that, when he mapped the brain for genital response, he found a "protrusion of the tongue was elicited" along a similar course. His examples of mammalian behavior are apropos. A certain type of monkey "instead of displaying erection . . . protrudes the tongue to the level of the forehead, both under conditions of threat and courtship." He also writes that "A noted American boxer was photographed" protruding his tongue as a type of display "upon being weighed in." Hair can also be used to challenge, especially since human males might once have had manes. MacLean, quoting Hingston, writes that "among primitive people the raising of the arm and showing the axillary hair is used as a threat. A hair tuft is part of the ensemble of a Scottish kilt." Adornment of the body itself can be used to challenge. Changes of appearance and exaggeration of size are characteristic reptilian types of behavior. MacLean writes:

> Apart from everyday examples provided by uniformed services, one can go to the very halls of learning for illustration, citing academic processions that, in addition to showy caps and gowns, are characterized by the somewhat stiff and off balanced swagger of the participants, giving the impression that everyone is out of step. Ironically, some will explain that the human inclination to 'dress up' is as *natural* as the desire to eat.
>
> (MacLean 1990: 233–4).

Submission

Submissive ("appeasement," "assertive") displays are conducive to survival because they signal compliance which could "serve to forestall, reduce, or terminate the punishing, and potentially deadly actions of a dominating animal." It seems that "certain aspects of submissive displays are so subtle and inconspicuous that an observer doubtless often overlooks them" (MacLean 1990: 112). Human beings may use submissive displays even more frequently than challenge (territorial) displays, with the result that they avoid unnecessary and potentially deadly conflict. This suggests that submissive displays are especially important to survival.

Courtship

Courtship and challenge displays resemble one another in a wide range of species. In some species, as MacLean points out, the struggle for territory is necessary prior to courtship, mating, and breeding. In blue spiny lizards, for instance, the female swishes her arched tail to display interest, and the male first performs a signature display. Then he enters into a courtship display "by a pushup and a series of head bobs performed while he lopes toward the female" (MacLean 1990: 110). MacLean remarks that the lizard's gait resembles that of a "close-in challenge display," which might give the impression of a hostile encounter. This mistaken impression is further confirmed when, as a part of the courtship display, the male nudges the female on her side several times and tries to bite her neck prior to mating. After mating, the male performs a number of actions while separating himself from the female that could either be marking or grooming behavior.

An attempt "to put together an ethogram on human courtship" might rely to a large extent on popular literature, the theater, and musical comedy. One instance of human courtship behavior is "the swagger and puffed-out chest of the male," and another is "the hip-swinging walk of the female." MacLean also cites a researcher who reports "one ubiquitous signal that he relates to flirtation among women and men . . . an upward jerking movement of the eyebrow as the person glances sideways" (MacLean 1990: 235). A certain "put-down" gesture, which seems to have a reptilian origin, can also be found in mammals such as apes and human beings, e.g. the rear-end display of the female. Chaucer's "Miller's Tale" gives a human instance.

Rigidification

Reptilian behavior is rigid, even compulsive, in the sense that it does what it has to do according to fixed patterns of repetitious, isopraxic, etc., types of behavior. Rigidification is beneficial to reptiles because it establishes patterns of behavior that promote social stability. There is, for instance, the reptilian "mannerliness" and "avoidance of bodily assault under ordinary conditions."

Hypostatizing

If reptilian power is united in a certain way with limbic emotion and neocortical reason, it can have the beneficial effect of "hypostatizing the sovereignty (the supreme power) of the law." This is beneficial when it fixes patterns of behavior that promote social stability and bring out the well-mannered lizard in them. It is beneficial when it inclines them to be like reptiles who seem "to have a built-in set of rules for maintaining mannerliness and avoidance of bodily assault under ordinary conditions" (MacLean 1990: 569). Human rigidification is harmful when it fixes destructive patterns of action and beliefs. The fact that a belief has been rigidified, even if it contributes to social stability, does not guarantee that it is good or true. Even the prejudices of the times can be rigidified.

Intolerance

Ironically, rigidified concepts that have a beneficial effect in promoting the well-being of our society can lead to intolerance. Human history is full of examples of rigidified damaging beliefs, such as racism, superstitions, class chauvinism, fanatical nationalism, intolerance, etc. MacLean suggests that the question of "neural mechanisms underlying an animal's response to what is alien or different" remains unanswered, but that it has important human implications "in regard to intolerance of aliens, blemishes, and the like" (MacLean 1990: 140).

MacLean warns that the population explosion and migration are likely to intensify this reaction and intensify nativistic hostility. Indeed, even in the relatively uncrowded conditions in which humans live today, many ethnic and racial groups struggle and fight over physical appearance, religion, and ideology. As we know, reptilian mannerliness breaks down and leads to combat in crowding. MacLean remarks that "the limbic system and neomammalian brain appear to have few 'built-in' mechanisms for dealing with crowded conditions" (1990: 138–41, 568–9). All of this suggests that urban crowding will cause the quality of human learning to deteriorate. Does this threaten the value of ideas available for rigidification?

Epilogue: critique of pure power

Power affects reptilian behavior in several ways. For instance, they use size to dominate each other. "Among lizards," as MacLean points out, "the spoils usually go to the animal of the largest size" (MacLean 1990: 235). Since reptiles also "seem to have an uncanny way of recognizing a larger animal," this leads the smaller ones to submit. As a result, different degrees of power also affect reptilian collective behavior and organization of social hierarchies.

Reptilian hierarchies promote order, and they are often maintained without doing violence to the individuals that constitute them. MacLean observes that submissive displays sometimes "serve to forestall, reduce, or terminate the punishing, and potentially deadly actions of a dominating animal" (MacLean 1990: 112). The result is that reptiles are inclined to use power "realistically" as a way of avoiding "bodily assault under ordinary conditions" (MacLean 1990: 569). The human use of reptilian power, however, does not always respect that kind of reptilian rationality.

Power could be defined as the ability to cause, prevent, or change something. This reptilian legacy gains positive or negative ethical significance in human beings depending on how they unite it with limbic emotion and neocortical reason, and accordingly how they use it. On the one hand, power is beneficial when human beings use it to prevent harm or change reality rationally. On the other hand, power is destructive when they treat it as the end, goal, purpose, and meaning of their existence. This produces an attitude of domination and submission that breeds vindictiveness and undermines egalitarian relationships. It disrespects truth and breeds authoritarianism in the same hierarchical structures needed for survival. Power loses its status as *means* and becomes supreme *end* and object of worship. The will to power, MacLean notes, deteriorates into "the draconian right of riding roughshod over other people" (MacLean 1990: 234).

Boundaries

The field within which power is exercised is a boundary. A species and individuals must establish and defend boundaries in order to survive. The territoriality of reptiles is "rational" in the sense that it promotes well-being and is a part of what MacLean calls their "mannerliness." Boundaries come to have additional meanings for human beings, since they can also designate the limits of the ego and fields of various kinds within which they exercise power. The human ego ought to have boundaries. Properly delimited egos are beneficial. Improperly delimited egos lead to the illusion of entitlement and intolerance. Human egotism distorts reality. Furthermore, the exceeding of boundaries can lead to the destructive expression of power. Rationally motivated behavior reestablishes proper reptilian boundaries over against egotistically destructive elaborations by the higher brain structures.

Rhythm and harmony

Reptilian order is both a kind of primal journey and primal music. The "temporal sequencing of behavior" that routinizes life and makes both ritual and precedent possible is *rhythm*; so too are the compulsive repeating of a specific act over and over again and the reenactment of meaningful activities. These sequences are integral to a certain *harmony* of reptilian life. The instinctive patterns of this order avoid violent confrontation whenever possible. The reptilian daily routine goes forth and returns to itself. It marks off a meaningful boundary because it limits power by not squandering it in destructive excess, just as Plato says a "musical man" must limit force when tuning a lyre. Power alone will break the strings, but force *limited by wisdom* will produce harmony.

Chapter 4

Conviction and conscience

Conviction, according to Paul D. MacLean, is the feeling that something, for instance a belief, is ultimately important regardless of whether it is true or not. This emotion, like other affects, comes from the limbic system and is therefore rooted in our paleomammalian heritage, even though its components would have to include higher brain functions. Conscience, the human sense of responsibility for life, comes from the relation between certain paleomammalian structures and the neomammalian pre-frontal lobes. A kind of harmony between limbic-based concern for offspring and the most recently evolved structures of the neocortex produces conscience.

The paleomammalian brain

The limbic system derives its name from Latin *limbus* because it forms a border around the brainstem. The limbic system, source of mammalian emotions, goes back 180 million years to old pre-primate mammals. MacLean pictures the first mammals as very small and perhaps nocturnal creatures. Like mammals that would yet evolve, their brains retained the earlier reptilian structures. But something new had also emerged. The cortices of their brains had expanded and differentiated to the point that they were no longer reptiles. The limbic system, which makes non-reptilian types of behavior possible, is the evolutionary result of "the progressive elaboration of the primitive cortex enveloping a large convolution which Broca called the great limbic lobe" (MacLean 1992: 61). MacLean believes that the limbic system distinguishes mammals from reptiles and enables them to interpret experience not in a merely compulsive reptilian way but in terms of "feelings that guide behavior required in self preservation and the preservation of the species" (MacLean 1990: 519).

General limbic affects

Unlike thoughts, limbic feelings are never neutral, but always have an unpleasant or pleasurable quality. External sensory systems produce specific affects, while basic affects arise from internal needs, such as "food, water, air, sexual outlet, sleep." General affects may be elicited either internally or externally. MacLean studies these affects mainly from the auras, peculiar modifications of consciousness, reported by an epileptic patient at the onset of a seizure, thinking that these abnormal states reveal a great deal about normal limbic emotions. The general affects are desire, fear, anger, dejection, gratulance, and affection. The last three are especially important in explaining conviction and conscience. Affection is related to carressive behavior and includes both the feelings of "sociability and mating" and the "feelings or sentiments related to parental behavior" to which I return later in this chapter.

Dejected feelings are associated with accidental or enforced separation from something to which one feels attached, as, for example, another person or group of people; an animal; an object; a place of abode; or something for which one was striving to obtain" (MacLean 1990: 444). Such feelings may also be caused by limbic epilepsy, as for example MacLean's patient who had a "feeling in the pit of the stomach that he characterized as a feeling of sadness and wanting to cry." Similar feelings include loneliness, homesickness, and depression. MacLean quotes researchers who claim that depressed feelings often accompany seizures of the type in question. Such feelings are characterized as a "sudden letdown of mood" and melancholy, ranging "from simple listlessness and apathy to agitated depression with suicidal attempts" (MacLean 1990: 444–5). At the same time, not all dejection is depression. The normal sense of guilt, vital to ethical experience, also seems to be a variation of dejection.

Gratulant feelings, in contrast to dejection, have a "pleasurable feeling tone," are joyous and can also be accompanied by "gratifying feelings associated with enhanced awareness, satisfying recognition, achievement, success, and discovery" (MacLean 1990: 445). Not all gratulant feelings are purely pleasant. They are sometimes followed by depression or can be mixed in an ambivalent way with unpleasantness. MacLean gives the example of the young man who said he had a "feeling of sadness which at the same time was somehow pleasant, like Juliet's 'sweet sorrow'" (MacLean 1990: 447). Visceral sensations tend to accompany gratulant feelings. For instance, MacLean quotes a report about a patient who said: "My fingertips began to vibrate thrillingly, and the sensation passed to my head, giving me the most ecstatic physical pleasure. Over and over, either by clenching my hands or by an effort of will, I reproduced this exciting, pleasurable stimulus in my head" (MacLean 1990: 447).

The range of gratulant feelings goes "all the way from mild satisfaction, to exultation, to ecstasy," according to MacLean. The milder side included feelings of completeness, contentment, elation, exhilaration, fascination, gladness, satisfaction, security, etc. Patients expressed states of exultation such as "well being of all the senses" and "a feeling like whiskey taking effect." The more ecstatic patients reported feeling eternal harmony, immense joy, intense happiness, and the like. Some said they experienced paradisical states, including feelings of "extraordinary beatitude," "as if in another world," "being in heaven," and "a wonderful feeling which gave the impression of lasting for hours" (MacLean 1990: 445–7).

Recognition can be a kind of gratulant limbic familiarity. This emotional state "carries along with it a feeling of gratification providing there is nothing threatening in what is recognized." *Déjà vu* , clairvoyance, and precognition seem to be variations of limbic familiarity. One patient reported that he had "familiar memories" when the surgeon stimulated the area near his uncus, and then believed he could "read the doctor's mind" when the interior region of his hippocampus was stimulated. Such stimulation can also cause future-directed recognition. A patient whose left temporal region was electrically stimulated said, "I knew everything that was going to happen in the near future . . . . As though I had been through all this before, and . . . I knew exactly what you were going to do next." Still another patient who was about to have a limbic seizure reported a feeling of extreme elation and also said "I am just about to find out knowledge no one else shares – something to do with the line between life and death" (MacLean 1990: 448).

Heightened awareness is still another kind of gratulant feeling. For instance, patients have reported that they have "clear bright thoughts" or a profound sense of discovery ("eureka" experience) when surgeons stimulate limbic structures. The sense of conviction is a type of gratulance, the belief that "things are more real" than ordinary reality or "the feeling that what is happening or what one is thinking at the moment is all important . . . revelation of the truth" (MacLean 1990: 448).

Conviction is a gratulant emotion, the feeling that our beliefs are "the truth and the whole truth," that they are "what the world is all about." On its own conviction cannot guarantee truth. A person can have conviction about truth, untruth, or something arbitrary. Conviction is rational if it attributes importance to scientific truth or a loving relationship, but irrational if it does this to superstition or egotism. It can also be arbitrary, as it was when a man allegedly swore that his salad was unconditional and absolute. MacLean quotes what a patient with limbic epilepsy said during an aura, the altered state of consciousness just before the seizure: "It was as though there were just everyday things going on as usual, only they seem so much more important and vital than they do in ordinary living." MacLean notes that conviction is no guarantee of certitude:

It is one thing to have the anciently derived limbic system to assure us of the authenticity of such things as food or a mate, but where do we stand if we must depend on the mental emanations of this same system for belief in our ideas, concepts, and theories? In the intellectual sphere, it would be as though we are continually tried by a jury that cannot read or write.

(MacLean 1990: 453)

Does the hippocampus have a role in conviction of self and reality?

The hippocampus, which literally means "sea horse" owing to its appearance, processes long-term memories. MacLean hypothesizes that it also contributes affect to what it processes. He suggests that it assimilates strangeness to familiarity and also has a vital role in producing limbic conviction, especially belief in self-identity and external reality.

The structure of the hippocampal formation enables it to synthesize the brain's two sources of information, one of which is internal and private and the other external and public. Conviction that the self exists, an abiding sense of self-reference, might depend partly on comparative fusion of the two sources and the memory's retention of it. MacLean suggests that the same process that preserves self-identity by retaining the past and anticipating the future also produces conviction that external reality exists. Furthermore, the way we view reality comes partly from paleomammalian emotion: "There is a saying that 'something does not exist until you give it a name' . . . unless it is imbued by an affective feeling, no matter how slight" (MacLean 1990: 516).

Conviction of self and reality depends upon the function of the hippocampus to process memories so that there will not be amnesia of ongoing internal and external experience. James Ashbrook amplifies MacLean's idea:

> Without that transformation of sensory input from an immediate present into a stabilized past . . . we have little sense of self and little orientation in time and space . . . . We then live in the hell of an eternal present, without the recent past and without a usable future.
>
> (Ashbrook 1989: 72)

Three subphases of limbic evolution

The hippocampus is intricately interconnected with three limbic subdivisions: amygdalar, septal, and thalamocingular (Figure 4). Each developed through a subphase of limbic evolution, the third of which marks the origin of ethical judgment. MacLean claims that "the two older

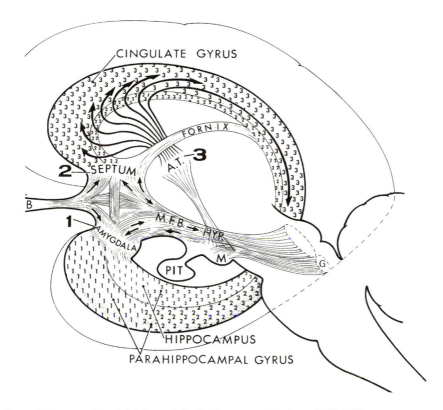

CINGULATE GYRUS

FORNIX

SEPTUM

A.T.

B

AMYGDALA

M.F.B. → HYP

PIT

M

G

HIPPOCAMPUS

PARAHIPPOCAMPAL GYRUS

Figure 4 Three main subdivisions of the limbic system (MacLean 1990: 315)

subdivisions associated with the amygdala and spetum are closely related to the olfactory apparatus" (MacLean 1992: 61).

Amygdala

This almond-shaped organ of self-preservation is not merely olfactory, but also oral, because it "is primarily involved in self-preservation as it pertains to behavior involved in feeding and the search to obtain food" (MacLean 1985: 412). MacLean points out that limbic seizures cause unpleasant feelings associated with the amygdala more often than they do gratulant feelings associated with other limbic structures. External social influences can trigger its rage. The amygdala seems to produce anger and hostile aggression as such. It bites and rips "flesh" of various kinds in many ways. Do amygdalas also use their owners' mouths for the verbal violence? Aren't needling, debunking, etc. just as oral as actual cannibalism? (See Chapter 7.)

Septum

This hedge-shaped organ of "sociability and mating" is olfactory, but not as oral as its more aggressive partner. MacLean suggests that the septum's "primal sexual functions" are beneficent and are potentially altruistic:

> A concern for the welfare of the species is based on sexuality. In the complex organization of old and new structures under consideration, we presumably have a neural ladder, a visionary ladder, for ascending from the most primitive sexual feeling to the highest level of altruistic sentiments.
>
> (MacLean 1962: 164)

Might the septum play some part in the desire that Eros inspires in lovers to ascend from the beauties of earth to the God-like essence of beauty in Socrates' speech? He claims to quote Diotima:

> He who has been instructed thus far in the things of love, and who has learned to see the beautiful in due order and succession, when he comes toward the end will suddenly perceive a nature of wondrous beauty (and this, Socrates, is the final cause of all our former toils).
>
> (Plato 1892: 210E)

Thalamocingulate

"Girdle wrapped around," the literal meaning of "cingulate gyrus," encircles the corpus colossum which, in turn, joins the two cerebral hemispheres. The term "thalamocingulate division," according to MacLean's classification, includes the cingulate gyrus and the fibers linking its inner cortical areas to the thalamus.

The cingulate gyrus coordinates autonomic functions. MacLean and others who study the brain's evolutionary development claim that the cingulate gyrus also produces cerebral activity that radically distinguishes mammals from reptiles. MacLean's 1985 essay, the most important text in his search for the source of beneficial limbic emotions, explains how parental affection, and ultimately conscience, originate from the thalamocingulate division. These structures gave rise to the "primal commandment," namely "Thou shalt not eat thy young or other flesh of thine own kind." Mammals have sometimes violated their commandment, but with the structures that emerged, perhaps millions of years ago, a new kind of life leapt into existence.

MacLean writes: "Experimental findings indicate that it is this thalamocingulate division that is primarily involved in the evolution of family-related behavioral triad – namely, nursing and maternal care; audio-vocal communication for maintaining contact; and play" (MacLean 1992: 62). *Nursing* might help explain the biological origin of altruism. He suggests that the neomammalian female's supplying milk to offspring is the biological origin of responsibility for the other. *Audio-vocal contact* is preverbal limbic-based communication between mother and offspring prior to language. "The separation call may represent the most primitive and basic mammalian vocalization . . . ." *Play*, a distinctly non-reptilian form of behavior, might have originally functioned "to promote harmony" in the mammalian nest. Play establishes good feelings and the possibility of getting something done without force. Other considerations include pseudo-fighting and play as a basis of culture (MacLean 1985: 413).

The neomammalian brain

The expanded neocortex of advanced mammals greatly increased their ability to perceive and respond to the external environment. MacLean compares this development to "the progressive enlargement of a central processor, providing an expanded memory and intelligence for increasing the chances of survival" (MacLean 1992: 65). Human neocortexes eventually developed asymmetrical hemispheres associated with handedness and speech. Late in evolutionary time, they gained the prefrontal cortex that generates a sense of the future.

I asked why we sometimes act rationally, according to MacLean's triune brain concept. The perceptive critic noted that "the organism with the most developed neocortex seems the least 'ethical' of all creatures. I wonder if the neocortex is not only the source of what's 'rational' but also of what's most 'irrational'" (Demas 1996). The truth seems to be that our neocortexes have made us capable of a new kind of rationality and a new kind of irrationality.

In 1949 MacLean explains rationally motivated behavior as neocortical override of more primitive impulses. We can be ethical because the "frontal lobes 'stand guard over' the visceral brain," namely "the id, the beast, or sin in man (e.g. gluttony, lechery, etc.)." Ruth Macklin takes this to mean that the "ego is in control of the id, whose behavior is dominated by reasoned judgment" (Macklin 1978: 176). Since at least 1985, MacLean has focused on how the primitive impulses contribute positively to rationally motivated behavior. As a result, acting ethically is not merely neocortical censorship over the brain's archaic heritage. Decision would be impossible without the neocortex, but our decisions, whether good or evil, have deeper evolutionary roots. Limbic emotions help determine the nature of neocortical override.

The guilt "fomented" by neocortical standing guard, as the 1949 essay terms it, might not be possible unless the limbic system had "already" bestowed the guilt that registers there. This could also be said of limbic conviction and parental concern for offspring. The same perceptive critic quoted a moment ago asks whether "the parental concern for offspring might be based on something more primitive and general" (Demas 1996). MacLean's answer is "yes," since primitive "paleopsychic" (sub-neocortical) processes originating in the limbic structures, basal ganglia, and even the cerebellum affect the frontal granular cortex. MacLean suggests that they may have a role in certain distinctively human types of behavior, including some that are clearly beneficial.

Crying and tearing

MacLean asks whether tearing might have emerged along with the use of fire, because smoke irritates the eyes. Fire handlers might have learned the danger of fire through non-fatal burns during the hundred thousand years or so in which the frontal lobes evolved. This could have given them the survival advantage over non-fire handlers who were burned up because they did not know the danger of fire. Those who handled it might have come to associate tearing with the mystique of fire, especially in the cremation of the bodies of loved ones. He wonders if this association helps explain why tears and crying are ways in which human beings identify with the feelings of others (MacLean 1985: 415 and 1990: 557).

Planning and a "memory of the future"

Our ability to remember a plan before executing it depends upon primitive brain structures as well as our frontal lobes. MacLean suggests that the cerebellum's link with the frontal lobes may contribute to their ability to calculate and plan. Projections from the thalamus into the granular cortex and various cortical association areas might help integrate memory of the past with awareness of what is presently happening. Planning something and remembering the plan seem to require that type of integration. The link between the frontal association cortex and the amygdala motivates planning for self, while its link with the thalamocingulate region through the medial dorsal nucleus motivates certain kinds of altruistic planning.

Empathy

We can identify with the feelings of others because the newest evolutionary parts of the neocortex are linked with archaic brain structures. The neurobiological basis of empathy is the fact that

> through its connections with the medial dorsal nucleus, the prefrontal cortex is the only neocortex that receives a strong projection from the

great visceral nerve. Presumably such internally derived experience is necessary for an individual's identification with the feelings of others. And it may be imagined that such an interiorized sense is also necessary for the "insight" requisite for the foresight to feel a concern for the future of others, as well as the self.

(MacLean 1990: 562)

Conscience

Two general limbic affects in particular call amygdalar selfishness into question. One is guilt and the other is affection. Parental affection, originally the female mammal's ethical responsibility to nurse offspring, becomes human responsibility for life. The medial dorsal nucleus is the neurobiological base of this elaboration because it connects the frontal lobes with the thalamocingulate region (Figure 5). As a result, "a parental concern for the young generalizes to other members of the species, a psychological development that amounts to an evolution from a sense of responsibility to what we call conscience" (MacLean 1990: 562). This statement culminates the ethical dimension of MacLean's triune brain hypothesis.

Self-reference

During a private interview at the Brain Behavior Laboratory on 12 June 1990, just as *Triune Brain in Evolution* was appearing, MacLean said he had

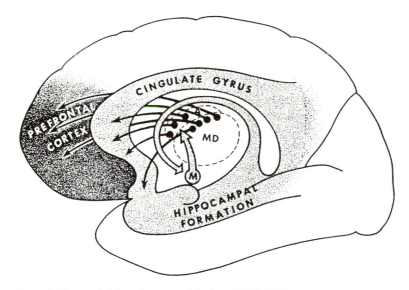

Figure 5 The medial dorsal nucleus (MacLean 1990: 535)

"introduced two Trojan horses" into that book, "conviction" and "self-reference." The second is an advanced product of the human neocortex. MacLean's understanding of the problem comes at least partly from J. Bronowski's reading of Kurt Gödel: "Many logical problems grow from this common root, namely that the range of reference of any reasonably rich system necessarily includes reference to itself. This creates an endless regress, an infinite hall of mirrors of self-reflection" (Bronowski 1966: 6).[1]

Referring to Bronowski's "infinite hall of mirrors," MacLean identifies the frustrating problem of self-reference which the neocortex creates but cannot solve:[2]

> Since the subjective brain is solely reliant on the derivation of imma-terial information, it can never establish an immutable yardstick of its own. Hence, for these reasons it is left with nondimensional space and nondimensional time for which it must arbitrarily set standards of its own. In this respect, it is saddled with a nonyielding relativity.
>
> (MacLean 1990: 571)

Epilogue: music

Play originates in the thalamocingulate region of the limbic system which we share with other mammals; therefore it is not uniquely human. However, our more developed neocortexes multiply the types of play of which we are capable.

Music is primal play with infinity, not the kind of infinity that frustrates. Music's infinity is totally different: it fulfills. It lets innocent rhythms like those of reptilian life be audible, harmonizes sublime and beautiful feelings with it in a pre-frontal rational architectonic infused with limbic conviction. This is the infinity of perfection. Musical rhythm and harmony thereby justify existence independently of the words that might or might not accompany them. Words are secondary because we can reduce them to the narrative rhythms and harmonies that are their meaning. Audible rhythm and harmony have already sprung from the source to which the words reduce.

Part three

At the threshold

Douglas Hofstadter finds what he calls "strange loops" in mathematics, graphic art, and music. These are processes that journey beyond, but also return to, their origins, referring back to themselves in spite of and partly on account of having been entangled in something different, external, and complex. They return home enriched by their adventure away from it. This return to self is similar to G.W.F. Hegel's "being-for-self," the process of restoring identity out of difference which he thinks lies at the heart of reality.

Chapter 5 explains Hofstadter's strange loops and his suggestion that they might be the crux of consciousness as a "self-reinforcing 'resonance' between different levels" of brain function. This seems to be closely related to Erich Harth's positive feedback biological model of consciousness. Chapter 6 examines biological hypotheses concerning consciousness that overtly or covertly incorporate similar self-referent models. Two examples are Francis Crick's "reverbertory circuits" and the biogenic structuralist suggestion of Eugene d'Aquili and others that "re-membering," or "bringing back together" is the "definitive characteristic of awareness." A still wider range of other biological hypotheses of consciousness might imply or be partly affected by self-referent models like resonance, reverberation, loops, reentry circuits, etc. This chapter also cites some models of consciousness that go beyond self-reference and, in doing so, clarify it.

Needless to say, these scientific models and the following interpretation do not claim to answer the question of how the brain becomes conscious. Suggesting that consciousness is "resonance" does not do this. Nor does saying that consciousness is a higher-level activity. None of these explains how the threshold is crossed. The threshold question remains unanswered, but the models of consciousness in the next two chapters suggest certain directions that might be important for empirical research and philosophical speculation. And there is increasing hope that science will eventually identify the physical processes that push brain events over into awareness. The perceptive critic asks: "What would be an example of becoming aware of a brain event? Are we ever aware of *brain* events directly?" (Demas, 1996). I answer that we are never aware of brain events, but some brain events are in a state of awareness: perception, memories, thoughts, feelings, etc.

"Consciousness," following Max Velmans, "is synonymous with 'awareness' or 'conscious awareness' (sometimes 'phenomenal awareness')." It is not to be equated with "mind," which is too broad a term since mind also includes non-conscious processing. "Self-consciousness" is too specific: "As one can be conscious of many things other than oneself (other people, the external world. etc.), this definition is too narrow." Similarly, "wakefulness" is not a synonym for consciousness: "When sleeping, for example, one can still have visual and auditory experiences in the form of dreams. Conversely, when awake there are many things at any given moment that one does *not experience*" (Velmans 1996: 2).

Paul D. MacLean once said in a private interview that consciousness might be "resonance at the submolecular level." A few years later, in the fall of 1997, when I thought I had finished Chapter 6, he published an essay I cite there in which he offers a few specific suggestions about this hypothesis. MacLean does not seem to change his position on the problem of self-reference in this essay. Chapter 5, however, argues that Hofstadter's theory of strange loops resolves that problem. What MacLean calls the "unyielding relativity" of self-reference does in fact yield at those moments when we view it as a strange loop returning to itself and thereby fulfilling itself. The frustrating relativity of a self-referential endless hall of mirrors is like incomplete music, but once fulfilled it becomes musical harmony.

Chapter 5

Self-reference and strange loops

Johann Sebastian Bach composed the *Art of the Fugue* about a year before he died. He based all 18 fugues in a single key on one "very simple theme in the most complex possible ways" and maintains the complexity "until the last *Contrapunctus*," according to Douglas Hofstadter.

Bach broke off the composition at that point, because his eyesight failed, and an operation to restore it blinded him; but as Hofstadter explains,

> This did not keep him from vigorous work on his monumental pro-
> ject, however. His aim was to construct a complete composition of
> fugal writing, and usage of multiple themes was one important facet
> of it. In what he planned as the next-to-last fugue, he inserted his own
> name coded into the notes as the third theme. However, upon this
> very act, his health became so precarious that he was forced to
> abandon work on his own cherished project.
>
> (Hofstadter 1980: 86)

Hofstadter asks the central question in connection with Bach's death, which followed soon afterwards:

> One day, without warning, Bach regained his vision. But a few hours
> later, he suffered a stroke; and ten days later, he died, leaving it for
> others to speculate on the incompleteness of the *Art of the Fugue*.
> Could it have been caused by Bach's attainment of self-reference?
>
> (Hofstadter 1980: 86)

Hofstadter's strange loops

Whether in music, graphic art, or mathematics, self-reference is a "strange loop." Bach's "Canon per Tonos" in *Musical Offering*, for instance, contains a strange loop:

> The "Strange Loop" phenomenon occurs whenever, by moving

upwards (or downwards) movement through the levels of some hierarchical system, we unexpectedly find ourselves right back where we started. (Here the system is that of musical keys.) Sometimes I use the term *Tangled Hierarchy* to describe a system in which a Strange Loop occurs.

(Hofstadter 1980: 10)

The graphic art of M.C. Escher (1902–1972) also contains strange loops, as his 1961 lithograph suggests:

Look, for example, at the lithograph *Waterfall* . . . and compare its six-step endlessly falling loop with the six-step endlessly rising loop of the "Canon per Tonos". The similarity of vision is remarkable. Bach and Escher are playing one single theme in two different "keys": music and art.

(Hofstadter 1980: 11–13)

Kurt Gödel's mathematical theorem also contains a strange loop which Hofstadter says appeals to the same "very simple and ancient intuitions" as the music of Bach and graphic art of Escher (Hofstadter 1980: 15). Hofstadter paraphrases Gödel: "All consistent axiomatic formations of number theory include undecidable propositions." The proof of this theorem "hinges upon the writing of a self-referential mathematical statement" in which *numbers* talk about number theory. Gödel's resulting strange loop is a mathematical version of the self-reference problem in the Epimenidean paradox: "Epimenides was a Cretan who made one immortal statement: 'All Cretans are liars.' A sharper version of the statement is simply 'I am lying'; or, 'This statement is false'" (Hofstadter: 1980: 17).

Strange loops sometimes conceal themselves by spreading themselves out over "several steps." For instance, Hofstadter turns the "one-step" strange loop in the version of the Epimenidean paradox I just quoted into this expanded version:

The following sentence is false.
The preceding sentence is false.

(Hofstadter 1980: 21)

Neither sentence is paradoxical on its own, but a strange loop comes into being in the way they point to one another when we "globally" put them together.

Escher's 1948 lithograph, *Drawing Hands*, is a graphic paradigm of that kind of expanded strange loop. It does not operate within "presumed level distinctions," for instance when "you're in the shower and you wash your left hand with your right, and then vice versa." Escher drew hands drawing one another. This strange loop is a tangled hierarchy:

> Here, a left hand (LH) draws a right hand (RH), while at the same time, RH draws LH. Once again, levels which ordinarily are seen as hierarchical – that which draws, and that which is drawn – turn back on each other, creating a Tangled Hierarchy.
>
> (Hofstadter 1980: 689)

This graphic violation of level distinctions is like language that talks about itself. Imagine a self-modifying chess game in which every move would "change the rules," then the new rules would "determine the moves," and so on "round and round the mulberry bush." In a tangled hierarchy, "something *in* the system jumps out and acts *on* the system, as if it were *outside* the system" (Hofstadter 1980: 688, 691).

Tangled hierarchies also have an inviolate level, which Hofstadter likens to "the vortex of the system, where all levels cross" and to an "Eternal Golden Braid". Bach's *Musical Offering*, for instance, contains a vortex in which many things go on at a number of levels, including "ingenious variations," "tricks," "original kinds of canons" (Hofstadter 1980: 713, 719). I say it is an impassioned interplay of thematic complexity and profoundest simplicity. Hofstadter says

> The *Musical Offering* is a fugue of fugues, a Tangled Hierarchy like those of Escher and Gödel, an intellectual construction which reminds me, in ways I cannot express, of the beautiful many-voiced fugue of the human mind. And that is why in my book the three strands of Gödel, Escher, and Bach are woven into an Eternal Golden Braid.
>
> (Hofstadter 1980: 719)

Hofstadter finds an inviolate level at the base of its tangled hierarchies in mathematics, graphic art, and music. His strange loops also help clarify other types of experience, including: the soul, free will, how to resolve the problem of self-reference (in the preceding chapter), and, most important, the nature of consciousness.

Our ability to produce symbols depends partly on our ability to symbolize ourselves, according to Hofstadter. He calls this ability the "self-symbol," a subsystem that functions like a "soul." It is a process by which the brain monitors itself, "communicating constantly with the rest of the subsystems and symbols in the brain, it keeps track of what symbols are active, and in what way" (Hofstadter 1980: 387). Furthermore, the brain also needs the self-symbol to situate bodily experience and to "make sense of the world surrounding a localized animate object." According to Hofstadter, free will is the activity of making choices by modeling situations in the world symbolically and ultimately our ability to symbolize ourselves as real. He says it causes us to be "sucked inexorably into interaction with the self-symbol, like a rowboat being pulled into a whirlpool . . . the vortex of the system, where all levels cross" (Hofstadter 1980: 338, 713).

Hofstadter's discovery of that vortex also resolves an outstanding problem attached to MacLean's hypothesis. The seemingly "unyielding" relativity of the problem of self-reference yields when self-reference passes beyond its alienated phase as an infinite hall of mirrors reflecting on itself and turns out to be what it truly is, namely self-recognition and ultimately our ability to symbolize ourselves as real. Self-reference is a dynamic process that *restores* itself to identity. It winds through tangled hierarchies and comes home to its starting point filled with meaning it did not have before it went forth.

Hofstadter's covert Hegelianism

This passage from alienated to fulfilled self-reference is also G.W.F. Hegel's movement from bad (spurious) to true infinity. Bad infinity is quantitative endlessness, including variations such as "monotonous alteration." This kind of infinity is based on the model of the endlessness beyond both limits of a *straight line*. It is "a flight beyond limited being which does not inwardly collect itself and does not know how to bring the negative back to the positive." By contrast, true infinity is "bent back into itself, becomes the *circle*, the line which has reached itself, which is closed and wholly present, without *beginning* and *end*" (Hegel 1969 [1816]: 149–51, 169). True infinity is *being-for-self*, the process by which something achieves its identity both in spite of and on account of its other. In order for something to be concrete, it has to journey forth from itself, figuratively speaking, and then return to itself, the *"consummation"* of *"qualitative* being" (Hegel 1969 [1816]: 157).

Strange loops as the crux of consciousness.

According to Hofstadter, something like "tangled recursion" might be the core of intelligence, including the artificial type, if we could devise "suitably complicated recursive systems . . . strong enough to break out of any predetermined patterns . . . programs which can *modify* themselves . . . which can act on programs, extending them, improving them, generalizing them, fixing them" (Hofstadter 1980: 152).

Consciousness emerges from the brain as a strange loop according to Hofstadter. He writes that, at least in principle, we might eventually be able to explain the brain processes of consciousness in a completely reductionist way. But he also suggests that such an explanation is likely to be incomprehensible owing to the complex nature of the explanation. In order "to translate it into a language we ourselves can fathom" we would have to "bring in 'soft' concepts such as levels, mappings, and meanings." Keeping this in mind, consciousness might arise as a certain kind of high-level function out of the jungle of neurons in the brain as "an interaction between levels in which the top level reaches back down towards the bottom level and influences it, while at the same time being determined by the bottom level . . . a self-reinforcing 'resonance' between different levels" (Hofstadter 1980: 709).

Hegel's qualitative leaps

The self-referential process of Hofstadter's strange loops that wind through hierarchies only to return to themselves, and in doing so produce the "self-reinforcing 'resonance' "of consciousness, is a type of Hegel's being-for-self. Consciousness is a new quality consummated in a leap that quantity alone cannot explain.

According to Hegel, quantitative limits can change "more" or "less" up to a certain point without turning something into a different quality, "when, for example, a field alters its limit it still remains what it was before, a field." Red is still red whether we change its quantity from bright to dull. By contrast, changing a qualitative limit immediately alters what kind of thing something is, for instance turning red into blue or a field into "a meadow, wood, and so on" (Hegel 1969 (1816): 186). Extraordinary amounts of quantitative change, however, can also change qualitative limits. Hegel asks

> does the pulling out of a single hair from the head or from a horse's tail produce baldness, or does a heap cease to be a heap if a grain is removed? An answer in the negative can be given without hesitation since such a removal constitutes only a quantitative difference, a difference moreover which is quite insignificant; thus a hair, a grain, is removed and this is repeated, only one of them being removed each time in accordance with the answer given. At last the qualitative change is revealed; the head or the tail is bald, the heap has disappeared . . . . the individually insignificant quantities (like the individually insignificant disbursements from a fortune) *add up* and the total constitutes the qualitative whole, so that finally this whole has vanished; the head is bald, the purse is empty.
>
> (Hegel 1969 [1816]: 335)

A new quality always emerges through a *leap*. Change in kind is always an absolute interruption:

the new quality in its merely quantitative relationship is, relative to the vanishing quality, an indifferent, indeterminate other, and the transition is therefore a *leap* .... Every birth and death, far from being a progressive gradualness, is an interruption of it and is the leap from a quantitative into a qualitative alteration.

(Hegel 1969 [1816]: 368–9)

Roland Fisher uses Hegel's model of qualitative change to suggest that the brain becomes conscious when "some prior physical process reaches a critical threshold" at which "Hegelian quantity – on the order of 10^{12} profusely interconnected neurons – is changing into a new quality: self-awareness or consciousness." He also characterizes consciousness as a "self-referential and self-observing quality ... capable of (recursively) observing its self-observations, i.e. interpreting change that is meaningful in relation to itself." This is analogous to "the feedback loop on a cybernetic control system that regulates and thus redefines (in our mind) the meanings of the whole in relation to the parts" (Fisher 1987: 5–6).

Epilogue: Harth's positive feedback

A story of a London pub known for its excellent stout metaphorically illustrates a similar self-referent model of consciousness, according to Erich Harth:

> The pub's reputation was the result of the concatenation of chance events and the mechanism of positive feedback that is often the cause of instability and novelty. The stout is always fresh because the pub is always crowded. The pub is always crowded because the stout is always fresh. Resulting also from this bootstrap process, which started with an all but untraceable fluctuation, was the sudden, unexpected prosperity of the owner.
>
> (Harth 1996: 611)

The brain might become conscious through a similar global self-referential loop, a cyclical biological process of "mutual interactions that allow the exchange of both bottom-up and top-down controls," an interplay of hierarchies in which "Microstructures are organized by macroscopic experience, and microscopic fluctuations are readily propagated upward" (Harth 1996: 611). This process depends on positive feedback.

Harth distinguishes between positive and negative feedback:

> The latter is a regulating or limiting mechanism. A thermostat is an example of negative feedback: If the temperature is too high, the source of heat is shut off; if the temperature is too low, the source of

heat is turned on. Negative feedback establishes conditions of pre-
dictability and stability. In positive feedback, by contrast, chance fluctuations are enhanced, instabilities exaggerated, often with explosive
consequences.

(Harth 1993: 67)

Allwyn Scott further clarifies the difference between the two types of
feedback by contrasting repeater amplifiers and oscillators. He writes that
long distance telephone transmission uses negative feedback "because it
stabilizes a system so the relationship between output and input (or effect
and cause) is fixed." By contrast, oscillators use positive feedback since
it "functions at the edge of instability, where the causal relationship
between input and output is about to be lost." This happens, for instance
when a public address system begins to "sing" in oscillation when "some
slight sound is picked up by the microphone, amplified, and returned to
the hall at a higher level that is self-sustaining. Generally such songs are
undesired" (Scott 1995: 133).

Global oscillations in the brain might also solve the two *binding problems*. The first is the difficulty of reconciling "the diversity of cortical processes with the apparent perceptual and individual unity." For instance,
why the "different sensory features of objects, though analyzed in different parts of the brain, are perceived as belonging to the same object"
(Harth 1996: 611, 619). The other binding problem is that of explaining the
"perceived unity of the conscious subject." Each of us has the "sensation
of being a unique and indivisible 'I,' the single receiver of all sensory
experiences past and present," planners of our futures. Daniel Dennett
(Chapter 1) and others argue that there is no central "I" and that no
"central meaner" or homunculus (imaginary person inside the head) of
any kind exists. Harth, also recognizing that there is no such fictitious
entity, responds that our sense of the unity of perception and self is
founded in the self-referent nature of consciousness. He writes that "we
now can view perception as a unitary process, in which central and per-
ipheral areas of the brain cooperate in a bootstrap fashion. The neural
message does not have to be read by any homunculus. It reads itself"
(Harth 1993: 71).

Harth's positive feedback model of consciousness brings the other concepts of this chapter together while they also answer MacLean's problem
of self-reference. These include Hofstadter's strange loops as the crux of
consciousness, Hegel's being-for-self as true infinity, as well as his and
Fisher's qualitative leap. If self-referent processes produce consciousness
in the brain, how do they do it biologically speaking? That is the question
of the next chapter.

Chapter 6

Biological loops and consciousness

All the hypotheses this chapter explains are exemplary for their naturalism and are either based on or incorporate self-referent models of consciousness. Those of Francis Crick (in collaboration with Christof Koch), Gerald Edelman, and Eugene d'Aquili (in collaboration with Charles D. Laughlin and John McManus) are explicitly self-referent. D'Aquili integrates a model of *symbolic* consciousness into his biological loop hypothesis in a way that brings us to one of the book's core questions: Why does the human brain symbolize *itself* as it does?

The hypotheses of Bernard Barrs and Roger Penrose indirectly rely on the self-referent model as a component of different ways of approaching consciousness. Furthermore, both Baars and Penrose argue that Plato's philosophy is relevant, but in different ways, to their respective physical approaches to consciousness. The chapter also refers to Paul D. MacLean's recent essay on consciousness.

Plausible model: Crick and Koch

The cogency of Crick's model of consciousness, built on his earlier collaboration with Koch, stands independently of the serious epistemological defects concerning religious and other symbols (Chapter 1). Crick's position is otherwise viable because it simultaneously opposes the solipsistic view that the world outside the brain does not exist, the behaviorist denial of consciousness, and the dualist denial that the brain produces it.

I believe that Crick is correct when he states that philosophy cannot explain how the brain is conscious. He claims that the structure of consciousness is presently hidden because science has not yet discovered it, not because it is unknowable in principle (as Colin McGinn thinks). Crick suggests his "plausible model" of consciousness, not as an answer to the question, but as a way to approach it experimentally: "Consciousness depends crucially on thalamic connections with the cortex. It exists only if certain areas have reverberatory circuits (involving layers 4 and 6) that project strongly enough to produce significant reverberations" (Crick 1995 [1994]: 252).

The plausible model seems to have two essential elements, the 40-Hertz hypothesis and the spotlight metaphor. He suggests that *lower cortical areas*, possibly the pyramidal cells of layer 5, might transciently express the results of activity taking place in various cortical areas, and that *short term memory* sustains that expression through a "reverberatory circuit from cortical layer 6 to the thalamus and back again to layers 4 and 6" (Crick 1995 [1994]: 251). As a result, *oscillations* synchronizing the spikes of "relevant neurons" typically with "rhythms in the 40-Hertz range" produce the attentional mechanisms of consciousness. The thalamus, he and Koch "surmised," produces a "spotlight of attention" and casts it selectively into the cerebral cortex:

> A common metaphor is that of a "spotlight" of visual attention. Inside the spotlight the information is processed in some special way. This makes us see the attended object or event more accurately and more quickly and also makes it easier to remember. Outside the "spotlight" the visual information is processed less, or differently, or not at all. The attentional system of the brain moves this hypothetical spotlight rapidly from one place in the visual field to another, just as, on a slower time scale, you move your eyes.
>
> (Crick 1993: 62)

Crick's model is especially paradigmatic because it bridges a potential gap between two models of consciousness, namely self-referent oscillation models like Harth's and Edelman's and Baars' "attentional scanning circuits" model, as it has been called (Hameroff and Penrose 1996: 507).

Theater model: Baars

Crick's spotlight metaphor might be an inadvertent neurobiological restatement of the fire in Plato's allegory of the cave that causes the prisoners chained in the dungeon to see shadows of things on the wall, according to Baars: "What is the difference between Plato's fire-cast shadows and Crick's thalamic spotlight?," Baars asks. He writes that he is "moved as much by the similarities as the differences: both are unifying conceptions of human consciousness. In fact, both seem to reflect the same underlying metaphor of our personal experience, the *theater metaphor*" (Baars 1997: 5).

According to Baars, this model signifies the source of consciousness as a "spotlight of attention" shining on "the stage of working memory." The metaphor points to a scientific hypothesis in which both the source of consciousness and most of its stage are unconscious. The hypothesis elements include reticular formation and specific nuclei of the thalamus to produce the spotlight and "one or more layers of cortex" as the stage. Working memory is on the stage, but it does not become conscious as long as it is not in the spotlight of attention. Consciousness initially arises at a limited point of *"convergence"* on the cortical stage when its contents are "limited to a brightly lit spot of attention," but then "conscious information *diverges*" and turns into a "global work space." Hence consciousness does not come from a "centralized command that tells neurons what to do" or arise at a "single point center" like the pineal gland or involve any other kind of Cartesian Theater that Daniel Dennett and others criticize (Baars and McGovern 1996, 89; Baars 1997: ix, 42–3).

Baars hypothesizes that an active biological loop hypothetically runs between certain parts of the cortex and their "corresponding thalamic relay nuclei" (Baars and McGovern 1996: 89) and that the very concept of global work space is self-referent because it is unitary. For instance, conscious and unconscious processes are globally united: "Conscious contents appear to be disseminated globally to a great multitude of networks throughout the brain that are unconscious, but that have observable conscious consequences downstream" (Baars 1997: ix). As a result, the theater metaphor has elements of the feedback model within it. The other side of this idea is that self-referent models of consciousness generally might require a metaphorical theater at the point of the loop's return to itself to clarify how the return is conscious.

The remembered present: Edelman

Consciousness emerges from "the evolutionary development of the ability to create a scene," according to Gerald Edelman. Primary consciousness is the "remembered present" that produces awareness of the scene, like an animal seeing "the room the way a beam of light illuminates it," he writes. Except for "that which is in the beam," he notes "all else is darkness" (Edelman 1992: 118, 122).

By contrast, secondary consciousness "adds socially constructed selfhood to this picture of biological individuality" because it allows consciousness to go beyond the primary "constraints of an immediate present," provides a symbolic memory and plans for the future. This "consciousness of consciousness" alters our relation to time: *"Freedom from time allows the location in time* of phenomenal states by a suffering or joyous self" (Edelman 1992: 133, 136).

Primary consciousness is the prerequisite of that more developed kind of self-consciousness. Understanding how the primary kind of awareness arises is the immediate question. Edelman writes that "At some transcendent moment in evolution, a variant with a reentrant circuit ... emerged. At that moment, memory became the substrate and servant of consciousness" (Edelman 1992: 207). This happened when the new circuit linked "value-category memory" and "global mappings."

Value-category memory

This kind of memory, which emerged as a novelty of evolution at an earlier time, already permitted us to structure external perceptions according to an internal categorical sense. Edelman calls this value-category memory and hypothesizes that it comes from "the *mutual interactions* of the thalamocortical and limbic-brain stem systems" (Edelman 1992: 119).

The limbic-brain stem system "evolved early to take care of bodily functions" and serves the "hedonic" and "physiological needs" of the interior life. Its "values" are adjusting to "evolutionarily physiological patterns." The circuits within this system are arranged in loops that "respond relatively slowly (in periods ranging from seconds to months)" (Edelman 1992: 117).

The thalamocortical system, by contrast, is "very fast in its responses (taking from milliseconds to seconds)." Edelman writes that "it does not contain loops so much as highly connected, layered local structures with massive reentrant connections." This system, which evolved later than the other one, connects the cortex with the external world through the thalamus, thereby making it possible to adapt to complex environments through new types of learning (Edelman 1992: 117).

Evolutionary changes eventually linked the two systems and produced value-category memory. As a result, the cortex could then structure external events against the "background" of inner adaptive values. This linking and the memory it produces is a necessary, but insufficient, explanation of our ability to bind events that are not causally connected with one another into a scene.

Global mappings

Primary consciousness, however, requires ongoing scenes of global mappings of "roughly contemporaneous events in the world" recursively interacting with one another through "a set of reentrant processes" (Edelman 1992: 119).

Global mappings, Edelman writes, are dynamic structures "containing multiple reentrant local maps (both motor and sensory) that are able to interact with nonmapped parts of the brain . . . includ[ing] . . . the hippocampus, the basal ganglia, and the cerebellum" (Edelman 1992: 89). Primary consciousness is between these ongoing mappings and value-category memory *before* "perceptual signals contribute lastingly to that memory." John J. Boitano, commenting on Edelman's position, writes that "primary consciousness results from the interaction in real time between memories of past value-category correlations and present world input as it is categorized by global mappings (but before the components of these mappings are altered by internal states)" (Boitano 1996: 116, 119).

The remembered present is conscious on account of various loops and reentrant processes, but decisively through the one just mentioned. Crick likens such explanations of consciousness to the idea that the brain is "talking to itself" when it, "after one or more steps, arrives back at its starting point." When he says that the problem with Edelman's position is "that it is difficult to find a pathway that is not reentrant" (Crick 1995: 234), he might be off track since Edelman's model of consciousness seems to depend mainly upon a specific reentrant process, namely the one that marks the hypothetical "transcendent moment of evolution." When he characterizes Edelman as "noted more for his exuberance than for his clarity" (Crick 1995: 284), *he fails to appreciate the possibility that the unique reentry loop of the remembered present and the 40-Herz oscillations that cause the attentional mechanisms of consciousness are kindred hypotheses.* Both of these scientists struggle with the self-referent nature of consciousness, and both hypotheses invite further testing.

Quantum orchestration: Penrose and Hameroff

Roger Penrose and Stuart R. Hameroff present a quantum model of consciousness that includes, but also goes beyond, normal self-referent biological models. They hypothesize that consciousness is the orchestration of a quantum process by microtubules within the cytoskeletons of the neurons of the brain.

Cytoskeletons and microtubules

The cytoskeleton of a cell not only holds it in shape but has a wider range of functions. For instance, the cilia a parmecium uses to swim are external continuations of its cytoskeleton. Penrose thinks that the cytoskeleton "seems also to contain the control system for the cell . . . providing 'conveyor belts' for the transporting of various molecules from one place to another . . . a combination of skeleton, muscle system, legs, blood circulatory system, and nervous system all rolled into one!" (Penrose 1994: 358). Microtubules, a part of the cell's cytoskeleton, are

> hollow cylindrical tubes, some 25 mm in diameter on the outside and 14 nm on the inside (where 'nm' = 'nanometer', which is 10^{-9} m), sometimes organized into larger tubelike fibers that consist of nine doublets, triplets, or partial triplets, of microtubules, organized in an arrangement with a fanlike cross-section . . . with sometimes a pair

of microtubules running down the center. The parmecium's cilia are structures of this kind.

(Penrose 1994: 358)

The microtubules are protein polymers made up of units called *tubulins,* each of which consists of a pair of *dimers,* "peanut shaped" protein structures of about 13 lattice-shaped columns running along the outside of the microtubules. They can exist in two different configurations, either straight or bent about 30 degrees towards the microtubule, depending upon which way an electron between the pair shifts. There is evidence that electrical polarization of the dimers determines the configuration by causing the shift.

Microtubules in neurons are relatively long and can extend the entire length of axons and dendrites. Among other things they can also "grow and shrink" and communicate with the microtubules of other neurons through *microtubule associated proteins.* Penrose asks if the tubulin dimers, rather than neurons, might be the basic computational units of the brain. If the answer is yes, then the brain is far vaster than previously supposed. The human brain might contain 10^{11} neurons, but every neuron is made up of about 10^4 tubulin dimers. Microtubules might be the site of quantum processes that produce consciousness.

Quantum coherence and reduction

Quantum theory holds that atoms and subatomic particles can behave like either waves or classical particles, depending upon certain conditions. Energy and mass are equivalent, according to the theory of relativity. Maintaining the wave state depends upon isolation: "As long as a quantum system such as an atom or subatomic particle remains isolated from its environment, it behaves as a 'wave of possibilities' and exists in coherent 'superposition' (with complex number coefficients) of many possible states" (Hameroff and Penrose 1996: 207). But in certain circumstances a wave state collapses into particles. There is considerable disagreement about what causes this to happen, but Hameroff and Penrose argue that a wave state can cause its own collapse, which they call "objective reduction." A wave inflicts this upon itself by "growing and persisting to reach a critical mass/time/energy threshold related to quantum gravity" (Hameroff and Penrose 1996: 507–8).

Different quantum processes can affect one another even though they are located in different places. For instance, reduction of one quantum process determines the outcome of any reduction of an entangled process,

which implies that all quantum objects that have once interacted are in some sense still connected! When two quantum systems have interacted, their wave functions become "phase entangled" so that when one system's wave function is collapsed, the other system's wave function, no matter how far away, instantly collapses as well. The nonlocal connection ("quantum entanglement") is instantaneous, independent of distance, and implies that the quantum entities, by sharing a wave function, are indivisible.

(Hameroff and Penrose 1996: 508)

Oscillations occur in the microtubules in a condition called "quantum coherence," when a quantum wave state "nonlocally links superpositioned tubulins." *Microtubule associated proteins* "act as 'nodes' that tune and orchestrate quantum oscillations," Hameroff and Penrose hypothesize. They also suggest that this computational activity in the brain produces pre-conscious and subconscious mental states (Hameroff and Penrose 1996: 526). Consciousness is integral to the collapse of quantum coherence in the reduction process.

Quantum coherence collapses within the microtubules when "the mass-energy difference among the superpositioned states of coherent tubulins critically perturbs space-time geometry." This reduction to a "single space-time" prevents the production of "multiple universes," according to this hypothesis. This collapse is abrupt, but not instantaneous. "Larger coherent sets will self-collapse faster, and smaller sets more slowly. Coherent sets that evolve over different time scales and in different brain distributions may be bound in an effectively simultaneous collapse." This kind of collapse "creates the instantaneous 'now'," while "Cascades of these events constitute the familiar 'stream of consciousness'." At the same time, consciousness is not merely the collapse of the wave state. It is *orchestrated objective reduction*. The same *microtubule associated proteins* that tune and orchestrate oscillations during quantum coherence also "help to orchestrate collapse" (Hameroff and Penrose 1996: 533). The resulting *orchestrated objective reduction* is consciousness:

On the view that I am tentatively putting forward, consciousness would be some manifestation of the quantum-entangled ... cytoskeletal state and of its involvement in the interplay ... [objective reduction] between quantum and classical levels of activity. The computer-like classically interconnected system of neurons would be continually influenced by this cytoskeletal activity, as the manifestation of whatever it is that we refer to as free will. The role of neurons, in this picture, is perhaps more like a *magnifying device* in which the smaller scale cytoskeletal action is transferred to something which can influence other organs of the body – such as muscles. Accordingly, the neuron level of description that provides the currently fashionable picture of the brain and mind is a mere *shadow* of the deeper level where we must seek the physical basis of *mind*.

(Penrose 1994: 376)

The orchestrated reduction called consciousness is non-computational, according to Penrose. It has qualities that computational systems lack, including aesthetic and moral judgments about the *beautiful* and the *good* "which require awareness and . . . a continuing controlling input from a sensitive . . . conscious – presumably human – presence" (Penrose 1994: 400–1). Since the nature of awareness is ability to apprehend such qualities, Penrose wonders whether orchestrated interplay that constitutes it might also be apprehension of Plato's forms. He asks:

> are the qualities of 'beauty' and 'goodness' *absolute* ones, in the Platonic sense in which the term 'absolute' is applied to truth – especially mathematical truth? . . . Might it be the case that our awareness is somehow able to make contact with such absolutes, and it is *this* that gives consciousness its essential strength? Perhaps there might be some clue, here, as to what our consciousness actually 'is' and what it is 'for'. Does awareness play some kind of role as a 'bridge' to a world of Platonic absolutes?
>
> (Penrose 1994: 401)

Once again, Crick seems not to appreciate the need for scientific diversity and intellectual pluralism when he characterizes Penrose as saying that "quantum gravity is mysterious and consciousness is mysterious and wouldn't it be wonderful if one explained the other?" He also states that "Penrose is a Platonist, a point of view not to everybody's taste" (Crick 1995: 283–4). It is important to notice that the quantum hypothesis of consciousness proposed by Penrose does not depend upon his Platonism, to which I return in Chapter 11.

Quantum resonance: MacLean

Paul D. MacLean's essay "The brain and subjective experience: questions of multilevel role of resonance" hypothesizes that the brain produces consciousness through a certain kind of quantum resonance. Claiming that the work of Penrose did not influence this concept, he explains the origin of his interest in resonance as the clue to consciousness:

> In 1948 I visited Dr James W. Papez, the well-known neuroanatomist and neurologist at Cornell University in Ithaca, New York. So as to answer some of my questions, he said he would like to perform a dissection of part of a human brain. During the quiet while he was

exposing the temporal region, I broke the silence by musing aloud, "What is the origin of subjective experience?" Raising his head and looking at me as if I would know, he answered in a single word, "Resonance!" That word has been resonating in my memory ever since.

(MacLean 1997: 147)

Resonance in general is "a reinforced vibration of a body exposed to another body vibrating at about the same frequency" (MacLean 1997: 157). MacLean uses the metaphor of musical harmony to illustrate the type of resonance that produces subjectivity:

Pendulums or tuning forks are used as favored objects to illustrate resonance mechanisms, but since later on I want to give emphasis to the harmonic aspects of resonance, I refer again to musical instruments. As familiar to musicians, plucking a full length string will give the fundamental tone (i.e., the lowest tone), together with a number of harmonic sounds that are multiple frequencies of the fundamental. As will be dealt with, harmonic resonance looms large in the consideration of subjectivity at the molecular and atomic levels both with respect to electrons ("matter particles") and photons ("electromagnetic particles") with their wave properties in relation to atoms.

(MacLean 1997: 157–8)

MacLean hypothesizes that consciousness depends upon resonance between proteins in the neurons, "both a receiving analyzer and a formulating emitter," comparing this to the saying that "it takes two to tango" (MacLean 1997: 157). He proposes that the decisive event causing this resonance is an *Aristotelian-type state of potentiality intervening between wave and particle states in quantum processes*: "In a sense, quantum mechanics has . . . provided us a ladder having two sides, with one side comprised of matter (i.e. particles) and the other side of measurable waves of energy, with immaterial information for rungs in between" (MacLean 1997: 162–3). The result is a "trialectical" model of quantum processes, consisting of wave, potentiality, and particle states. MacLean hypothesizes that the resonance of consciousness comes from the juncture between the first and the third states.

Restating MacLean's problem of self-reference in terms of strange loops that also return to themselves might clarify the nature of the resonance that MacLean suggests produces consciousness. Even though he does not make this connection, his resonance is at least covertly fulfilled self-reference. Resonance is a type of oscillation. Furthermore, the analyzing protein receiver must have a relation to itself through the formulating protein emitter and the emitter through the receiver. Making this explicit would tend to bring MacLean's proposal about consciousness into the main stream of manifestly self-referent biological hypotheses cited in this chapter and the preceding one.

Re-membering: Laughlin, McManus, d'Aquili

These scientists (henceforth "LMD") refer to MacLean's research and build upon his triune brain concept. They use a method called "biogenic structuralism," a radical synthesis of neuroscience, phenomenology, and anthropology. LMD study the anatomy, physiology, and organization of the brain in search of the biological base of a wide range of experiences, including symbols and their mythical elaborations. Furthermore, they propose a biological explanation of consciousness, integral to their theory of symbols, which is manifestly self-referent.

The nervous system basically serves the need to adapt, according to LMD. It does this by regulating and processing sensory information, producing and testing models of reality, and assigning action conducive to adaptation. Brains make this possible by mixing neural circuits when they *link* them with other circuits through complex hierarchical patterns. Consciousness is integral to this *linking* process: "This linking up of neurons to form networks, and networks to form more complex networks and models is a process known as *entrainment*" (LMD 1992: 52–3). "Warps" *disentrain* these links, but *reentrainment* restores them into what Hegel calls being-for-self. LMD give us a scaled-down model of a globally complex neurobiological process to illustrate "reverberation," writing that

> neural models function by means of patterned activity over time; that is, they are four-dimensional structures. We might imagine a wave of activity, or *reentrainent*, among the cells making up a model, an activity having a beginning, a series of transformative phases (discrete entrainments, disentrainments, and reentrainments), and an ending. This sustained and patterned activity is called *reverberation*.
>
> (LMD 1992: 58)

We experience consciousness as a stream even though it is a neurobiologically discontinuous process. Brains "re-member" the chunks of sensation through a process that resembles Hofstadter's strange loop and similar self-referent models. Furthermore, "re-membering . . . is the definitive characteristic of awareness." It restores self-reference by bringing the chunks of sensation "back together" in a certain way. Sensation actually "appears in chunks" which come to us in *phases*, while *warps* stand between the perceptive episodes of the phases and separate them. Reverberative circuits also run through the warps, connecting prior and subsequent phases. This mediates cognitive material between them: "During the warp the most rapid, abrupt, and causally efficacious reentrainment of neural networks mediating consciousness occurs." The process of reentraining neural networks across the warp and re-membering the neural structures is consciousness: "The material literally must be 're-membered' ('re-collected,' 're-called'); it is reconstituted in the succeeding phase. Re-membering, or 'bringing back together,' is the definitive characteristic of awareness. Indeed, consciousness *is* a type of re-membering" (LMD 1992: 151).

Epilogue: consciousness as symbolic

Symbols can affect the way in which the brain re-members neural structures and their cognitive material, and these structures also make it possible for us to have symbolic experiences. As a result, consciousness is "essentially a symbolic process." A *symbol* is a stimulus (external or internal) that signifies a *meaning* which "may or may not be isomorphic with the event in reality" that evoked it. That meaning is the whole of which the symbol is the part that serves as its vehicle: "*The symbolic process is that function of the nervous system by which the neural network mediating the whole is entrained by and to the network mediating the part*" (LMD 1992: 163, 335).

Brains typically generate myths to narrate the symbolic process. Myths come from the brain's innate "prepared recognition" of certain relations, according to d'Aquili in a statement obviously based on MacLean's work when he writes that "this integrated evolution of the brain may have resulted in primitive stereotyped thought patterns arising from the earliest development of the neocortex out of the paleocortex and subcortical structures" (d'Aquili 1986: 142–3). Furthermore, this process which is "governed by the neocortex" might also be based on "direct neocortical-limbic connections" (d'Aquili 1986: 155). Referring to MacLean's triune brain concept, d'Aquili writes:

> We must keep in mind that these ancient parts of the brain mediate not only emotional discharge but, more anciently, both physiological homeostasis and the repetitive and rhythmic motor behavior . . . the earliest glimmerings of what would be recognizable to us as thoughts may have arisen out of, and in intimate juxtaposition to, the repetitive and rhythmic behavior that goes back to our premammalian ancestors. It should not be surprising, therefore, that such thought might be stereotyped and repetitive in character, and that mythic themes have a general and universal character.
>
> (d'Aquili 1986: 143)

Myth production also depends on the same six "cognitive operators" the brain uses to process sensory input and organize experience either factually or symbolically. Each of these functions, d'Aquili hypothesizes, might be mediated by a specific neo-cortical structure.

Two cognitive operators especially dominate myth production. The *binary operator*, which might be linked with the inferior parietal lobule, produces meaning "by ordering abstract elements into dyads involving varying degrees of polarity so that each pole of the dyad derives meaning from contrast with the other pole." These dyads include: "inside–outside, above–below, left–right, in front–behind, all–nothing, before–after, and simultaneous–sequential." These polarities get their significance from their opposition to one another when the brain produces myths. The *value operator* assigns "an affective valence" to the polarities the binary operator produces. It does not do this according to an absolutely fixed pattern, since any of the alignments can be reversed, but "'within' is usually defined with good and 'without' with bad" (d'Aquili 1986: 149).

Part four

Vacuum in a bubble

The Epilogue narrates the story of how the strange metaphor of the vacuum in the bubble originated and suggests why it has haunted me most of my life. The next two chapters explain what it means. This metaphor characterizes the darkest part of the mystery of the human brain, including some of the odd ways in which we symbolize the brain and dread its extreme fragility. *Vacuum* stands for the opacity of the brain's way of symbolizing itself and *bubble* for its dreadful vulnerability.

Opacity

The vacuum of opacity is our inability as human beings to come to terms with even our limited scientific knowledge of the brain; and knowing how limited this knowledge is escalates the mystery. We cannot appropriate the fact *that* consciousness comes into existence inside the three pound pulsating mass inside our heads, quite apart from the question of *how* it does. The thought that the brain of each of us is a cosmos of interconnected neurons (and microtubules!) is overwhelmingly opaque. At the same time, the brain's strange opacity in thinking about itself seems to have pre-scientific roots. Many ancient and archaic people already knew that the brain was the organ of consciousness. Being-for-self runs amuck when brains try to focus on the existential implications of what they are. This frustration of self-reference can take various shapes, ranging from haunting fascination with brains to dread of them.

The brain's encasement in the head might contribute to its mystique. The head is the most prominent part of the *self-symbol*, Douglas Hofstadter's term for what marks off the individual's identity "in relation to the other objects around it" (Hofstadter 1980: 338). Those objects are *without*; the brain is both literally and mythically *within* the body's least penetrable fortress, to use Eugene d'Aquili's terms.

Fantasies about what (or who) might be in the center of the head have haunted many. The homunculus myth is one of the brain's oddest ways of symbolizing itself and its container. Francis Crick pictures an homunculus as "An imaginary person within the brain who perceives objects and events and makes decisions" (Crick 1995: 274). William Calvin describes it as a

> 'little person inside the head,' the conductor of our cerebral symphony, who contemplates the past and forecasts the future, makes decisions about relative worth, plans what is to be tomorrow, feels dismay when seeing a tragedy unfold, and narrates our life story.
> (Calvin 1990: 3)

Does the brain invent homunculus myths *only* after it starts figuring out how it functions or is there some more biologically determined reason that brains invent myths about what is *within* the head?

Plato's *Timaeus* calls attention to the head as surrounding the brain. The theological mythology at the base of this dialogue also pulls Platonic dualism somewhat towards monism, and in doing so cracks the dualistic container a little. The Creator himself molds the brain to contain the soul and the head to contain the brain:

> And that portion of the marrow which was intended to receive within itself, as it were into a field, the divine seed He molded in the shape of a perfect globe and bestowed upon it the name of "brain," purposing that when each living creature should be completed, the vessel surrounding this should be called the "head."
>
> (Plato 1975: 73C–D)

Hofstadter's self-symbol and the strange loop running through it might be the functionalist counterpart of such a myth:

> All the stimuli coming into the system are centered on one small mass in space. It would be a glaring hole in a brain's symbolic structure not to have a symbol for the physical object in which it is housed, and which plays a larger role in the events it mirrors than any other object.
>
> (Hosftadter 1980: 388)

Questions like these must have been haunting me in 1991 when I reflected on the fact that brains are located behind our faces:

> Brains differ from other vital organs not only anatomically, but also in terms of what they represent. Faces surround them and eyes are external extensions of the brain. At the same time, the face and eyes are organs by which one is recognized and identified. They are instruments of personal identity and its expression. Head injuries that damage the brain often disfigure the face. Surgical access to the brain usually means opening the head. The organ of self-identity ironically happens to be housed behind the face, which is the most obvious visible symbol of self-identity.
>
> (Keyes 1991: 129)

Vulnerability

The bubble of vulnerability is the brain's extreme fragility. It is disturbing to realize that the cosmos within our heads is mortal and, even while alive, can be easily attacked. The next two chapters introduce conflict and discord into the rhythm and harmony of *Brain Mystery Light and Dark* and deliberately contain almost no hint of how the last three chapters will restore them. Chapter 8 tells the story of the brain injury of neurologist A.R. Luria's patient, meditates on it, and concludes by exposing some other "wounds of negativity" in the heart of brain mystery. Chapter 7 prepares the way; following a clue from Calvin, it explains how a number of different things, ranging from rocks to words, can easily penetrate brains.

Throwing things

William H. Calvin hypothesizes that handedness and the language centers of the brain might have evolved as they did through throwing things. He suggests that these developed in the left hemisphere because human beings became skilled using their right hands in the "ballistic movements" required for hunting. Throwing preceded language and established the "sequencing specialization" that makes it possible:

> Maybe it was throwing rocks at prey that got the brain started on the road to lateralization and language. So maybe that's why throwing is so important to human evolution: advanced pitching is distinctly a one-handed operation . . . . So perhaps language was built on the scaffolding of sequencing rather than snarls . . . throwing could have enlarged the brain faster than intelligence.
>
> (Calvin 1983: 35, 40)

Could the same throwing that enlarged the brain of the thrower often have aimed at the brain of the prey? If so, might this strange paradox show us something raw and primitive about the intentionality of harm? According to Calvin, a quicker way to kill a prey is to throw things at its brain from a distance rather than chase it; and long range throwing is easier and safer for the hunter.

Types of projectile

The best "way to get range is to throw a smaller rock with one hand" and swing it before throwing it, "nature's version" of the sling that "David used on Goliath" (Calvin 1983: 31).

Bullets

"High velocity," according to Calvin, "is better than massive weight – so the current M-16 army rifle now uses a small .22-caliber bullet with lots of power behind it" (Calvin 1983: 31). A.R. Luria gives an account of how a piece of shrapnel in war destroyed the overlap of the parietal, occipital, and temporal lobes of the brain of a soldier named Zaretsky. Since other parts of his neocortex, including his pre-frontal lobes, were completely untouched, he was tragically aware of his condition. Luria preserves Zaretsky's words and weaves them into a tragic masterpiece in *The Man With a Shattered World: The History of a Brain Wound*. He quotes Zaretsky who asks what the human condition would be "if it were not for war." Zaretsky contrasts the ease with which we imagine the flight of space ships with our unwillingness to think of that of bullets in war:

> As for the flight of a bullet, or a shell or bomb fragment, that rips open a man's skull, splitting and burning the tissues of his brain, crippling his memory, sight, hearing, awareness – these days people don't find anything extraordinary in that. But if it's not extraordinary, why am I ill? Why doesn't my memory function, my sight return?
>
> (Luria 1972: xxi)

Bludgeons

"Chimps," according to Calvin, "have been observed using both arms overhead to throw a stone down at the head of a dead monkey, trying to break open the skull." He continues with a cynical sentence fragment and asks, "Also in aid of extracting a delicacy food (were brains the original *pièce de résistance*?)" (Calvin 1983: 29). One wonders how many other images Calvin has in mind but does not share with us:

> Think back to that chimp, trying to brain that dead monkey. Suppose the monkey wasn't dead; braining it would make it safe for eating. One doesn't want to get too close to a wounded animal thrashing around . . . . So keeping a safe distance away and throwing stones at its head would have been a useful practice, keeping oneself healthy and one's offspring fed. Just move stone throwing up to the beginning, rather than waiting for desert time.
>
> (Calvin 1983:31)

Vincent Zigas (1990) describes a bizarre ritual in which a tribe of human beings ate the brains of the deceased, hoping to keep in contact with them, only to be stricken with "kuru" ("laughing death"). The thought of brain cannibalism, however, is not limited to such tribes. It also has a niche in American popular culture, for instance in some videotapes obtainable in neighborhood convenience stores. Is this merely a symptom of a culture that seeks new vistas of grossness for profit? Of course the profiteer can always say "What offends one person entertains another. Beauty is in the eye of the beholder." Or has cultural decadence accidentally dug up a recurrent symbol? What follows does not depend on how we answer the question, since it is "only" about mind cannibalism.

Words

Let's push Calvin's hypothesis to its rightful limit. Why not throw language, rather than rocks, at the brains of prey? Words are invisible, and they penetrate heads through ears; and the thrower gets by with it because it's legal. Certain combinations of words thrown at the "right" time and in the "right" way can wound and destroy brains. If we are consistent monists, steadfast in saying that brain and mind are one, then it is clear that verbal ballistics are nothing but the mental counterparts of bludgeons and bullets.

Types of mind cannibalism

Egotists try to reduce the other to their own use, puff themselves up with great solemnity, and use verbal ballistics to hunt their prey, steal its life, and feed on it. They craft words as utensils to eat their victims in a power play that hovers, metaphorically speaking, between rape and cannibalism. These mind cannibals are also brain eaters in the sense that brain/mind are identical. They simply enter their victims' brains differently. They have the illusion that they are entitled to transgress the boundary between "within" and "without" to gorge on stolen life. This verbal ritual can be crude in disarmingly sophisticated ways. I base the following varieties of mind cannibalism on my earlier analysis of the four types of everyday language of degradation (Chapter 2) which I elsewhere call "elite crudity" (Keyes 1989: 16).

Needling

This word characterizes the same kind of degradation both here and in my 1989 account. It is the same as Erich Fromm's verbal sadism:

> Mental cruelty, the wish to humiliate and to hurt another person's feelings, is probably even more widespread than physical sadism. This type of sadistic attack is much safer for the sadist; after all, no physical force but "only'" words have been used.
>
> (Fromm 1973: 317–18)

The ballistics of needling, if I may twist the metaphor somewhat, are easy, legal, and so widespread that they are conventional. As Fromm points out, it is an easy kind of torture to conceal:

> Mental sadism may be disguised in many seemingly harmless ways: a question, a smile, a confusing remark. Who does not know an "artist" in this kind of sadism, the one who finds just the right word or the right gesture to embarrass or humiliate another in this innocent way.
>
> (Fromm 1973: 18)

Skilled needlers conceal their sinister work so effectively that they even make their victims "deny the existence of the insult while inflicting it," as I explain.

Needling has two other peculiar characteristics. *Gradualness* is the needler's control of the quantity of verbal cruelty in order to keep the relationship intact. It is the kind of "deliberate understatement" that aims at staying just below the victim's "explosive threshold" in order "to deliver the poison in small doses." Furthermore, pausing gives old wounds time to fester. *Variability* is changing the kind of verbal ballistics in order to keep the prey off guard. Victims are so ready to protect their old festering wounds that they are unprepared for what comes next if the trajectory is completely different. Of course, if a victim ever confronts a needler with any of this, he invariably says he was only kidding. "Can't you take a joke?" (Keyes 1989: 34–7).

Scavenging

A "scavage," according to *The Oxford English Dictionary*, is a "toll formerly levied by the mayor, sheriff, or corporation of London and other towns on strangers, on goods offered for sale within their precincts." A scavenger is "An officer whose duty it was to take 'scavage,' and who was afterwards also charged with the duty of keeping the streets clean." A "scavenger's daughter," however, is an "instrument of torture" (*Oxford English Dictionary* 1989: 14, 601–3).

Scavenging, as I use the word here, is needling to poke meaning out of the victim's mind. As I note elsewhere, "We cannot easily know the system by which our values nourish us, but our Needlers make it their object to know this" (Keyes 1989). Scavenging also includes "debunking" and "levelling." The former uses fallacious language to poison what the victim values to turn it into a "sickened version of itself." The latter lowers "anything interesting to a state of unimportance" (Keyes 1989: 3). Even though levelling is collective and not mainly something individual persons do, as Kierkegaard knows, it produces stereotypes that serve as ready-made tools of scavenging.

Scavengers knowingly or unknowingly scramble their prey's ability to apprehend the values that give life meaning. To scavenge is to brain his or her thesis, no matter what it is, with some crudely shaped antithesis. Such bludgeons include levelled stereotypes, conventional ideologies, and informal fallacies. Consider this illustrative, but relatively less subtle, instance of how a scavenger "blames Marx for Stalin, blames Christ for the Inquisition, and forgets that other grounds besides Marx lay behind Stalin and that other grounds besides Christ lay behind the Inquisition" (Keyes 1989: 78).

Scavenging shoots that "part" of the mind that holds value systems together and makes them accessible. It blocks the rhythm and distorts the harmony that constitutes an intellectual intuition. It dissociates the parts and discredits each separately for not meaning anything on its own. Is a single note isolated from a Bach fugue supposed to mean something on its own? Scavenging fosters irrelevant associations and realigns the fragments according to a pattern that distracts from the original meaning. This kind of verbal torture at least temporarily fragments the victim's ability to grasp meaning similar to frontal lobe injuries. Judith Hooper and Dick Teresi (1986: 41–2) cite A.R. Luria's report of a patient who "becomes so distracted by irrelevant stimuli that he cannot carry out complex actions" because "uncontrollable floods of inert stereotypes" overwhelmed them. When Luria asked one patient to light a candle "he struck a match correctly but instead of putting it to the candle . . . he put the candle in his mouth and started to 'smoke' it like a cigarette" (Luria 1973: 199). Here is another example:

> A patient with a frontal lobe lesion is shown the picture of a man who has fallen through the ice. People are running towards him in an attempt to save his life. On the ice, near the hole, is a notice 'danger.' In the background of the picture are the walls of a town and a church . . . . Instead of analysing the picture he sees the notice 'danger' and immediately concludes: 'the zoo' or 'high voltage cables' or 'infected area.' Having seen the policeman running to save the drowning man, he immediately exclaims: 'war,' while the walls of the town with the church prompt the explanation 'the Kremlin.' Analysis of the picture in this case is replaced by elementary guesswork, and organized intellectual activity is impossible.
>
> (Luria 1973: 214–16)

Scavengers verbally simulate effects like these in their victims' ability to integrate and apprehend their value systems. Scavenging is sophistical distraction and therefore completely different from rational criticism of beliefs which examines them logically.

Psychizatry

Sarcasm is literally "flesh ripping." Similarly Dan, whom I identify in a moment, later coined what he calls the deliberately ugly word "psychizatry" to mean "soul ripping." It is the opposite of "psychiatry," which means "soul healing." Psychiatrists, like all physicians, are bound by the rule "first do no harm." Pointing out that some psychiatrists have violated this rule intentionally or unintentionally and committed psychizatry *is not a criticism of psychiatry as such*. It is only a judgment against the particular type of it, possibly more prevalent in the US than elsewhere, that explicitly or implicitly views mental health as conformity to the popular culture.

A psychizatrist (PZ) tears souls apart by scavaging them with certain "therapeutic" bludgeons. These include crude type casting and enforcing conventional stereotypes, inert or otherwise. If patients do not react to the scavaging, their acceptance of its content is presumed. If they do try to challenge it, the PZ *always* says: "Your over reaction proves you accept it." This trap turns patients into prey. So does alleging that *every* action and *all* its side effects have an unconscious, but nevertheless deliberate, motivation. Furthermore, PZs are held to be infallible. This illusion of infallibility is attributed by somebody else and is presumed by the PZ.

Only twice in my life did I ever hear anyone attribute infallibility to an entire group of persons. Insisting that nothing the disputed group does can be questioned seems to be another way of saying that whatever appears is absolute. Both of the following attributions show that even well-educated and intelligent people can fall victim to scavenging.

The first was at a conference on the education of children at Harvard in 1977. Someone said with obvious humility that "one problem with our public schools is that some groups place a higher priority on improving teachers' working conditions than on educating children." Despite the fact that the statement was not inflammatory, a Harvard education professor nonetheless vehemently responded: "You must never criticize any labor union under any circumstances. What labor unions do is always totally correct. They are all totally beyond criticism." The professor was clearly not joking.

The second attribution of infallibility happened in Pittsburgh about ten years later. I made the mistake of telling a friend whose judgment I had trusted that psychiatrists sometimes make mistakes. He was not an MD, just as the Harvard professor was not a public school teacher, yet he spoke with the same kind of unquestioning conviction: "Psychiatrists never make mistakes. Everything they say is right. The patient can never go beyond it, but only relate to it."

There is a story, which I hope is not true, of a man who told his "psychiatrist" that he felt like killing himself. The "psychiatrist" allegedly answered "Go ahead." As a result, the patient jumped out the window, but instead of dying, he remained paralyzed for life. Hypothetically grant that this actually happened, and calling it a mistake would be tragic understatement. Dan is a fictitious name for an actual patient who suffered much from having his soul professionally ripped. Unlike the man who jumped, he survived his PZ by not attributing infallibility to him. Also unlike the earlier story, I know that Dan's lamentation is factual.

Epilogue: the lamentation of Dan

He came from the western part of the US partly to discuss aesthetics with me, seeking a philosophical grasp of his deep involvement in music and literature. Eventually we confided in one another. Dan read and criticized the Epilogue of this book, with the result that my metaphor of the "vacuum in a bubble" inspired his nightmare of the brain in a vat at the end of the next chapter.

Dan invented the word "psychizatry" in connection with what he laments, which predates his dream and is essentially unrelated to it. His lamentation is the account he gave me of his unfortunate experience with two different "psychiatrists" between 1979 and 1983. Dan had undergone a humiliating defeat trying to preserve the musical tradition of a certain institution. Being forced to capitulate to the "popular culture" precipitated an agitated depression reaction. The first physician irreparably harmed him by trying to turn him into a "conventional conformist" and finally telling him to compromise with the popular culture: "Select what you like in it and ignore the rest." This psychiatrist then blocked Dan's attempts to challenge the advice and tried to make him take haldol, a powerful dopamine suppressant. Dan says that this psychiatrist probably harmed him inadvertently, but he likens the damage to what Nietzsche's Zarathustra says about a hermit being like a well. It is easy to throw a stone into it but impossible to pull it out. That drove Dan deeper into depression.

The second "psychiatrist" tore Dan's soul by trying to make him ignore the harm the first had done. He worked at covering up the other one's blunder with fervor similar to that of the professor who said that no trades union can ever be criticized. This PZ volatilized the inadvertent mistake of the first by attributing infallibility to it. He used all the "therapeutic" bludgeons listed above on Dan and also needled him about his religion, which made Dan terminate "therapy." He chided Dan for being "too intellectual" and not in touch with his feelings. Then when Dan expressed his feelings, the PZ said he was "overly emotional." Once Dan hesitated to talk about a dream, and the PZ said "It's only a dream. Go ahead and tell it." Dan told it, and the PZ scoffed at the dream's content. Worst of all, he repeatedly tried to break up Dan's most basic human relationship. Dan quotes verbatim one comment that he snarled: "What's love? It's nothing but a man's illusion that one woman is different from other women."

Dan's lamentation has a comic outcome. He recovered from his depression by seeing a general practitioner who asked no questions about his personal life other than symptoms, but simply prescribed the right antidepressant. While taking the drug, he decided to do the opposite of most of what both "psychiatrists" demanded. As a result he no longer needs the drug.

Chapter 8

Brain dread

Burning shrapnel crashed into Zaretsky's head on 2 March 1943, when he was defending the Russian front against Nazi invaders. The brain injury devastated his mind, even though he survived. It destroyed the right half of his vision of everything, including his own body. It also fragmented his ability to analyze, synthesize, and organize his own thoughts into coherent patterns. In spite of this, he struggled courageously for several years to remember and write down what had happened, even though he could not recognize his own words.

Meditation on Zaretsky

A.R. Luria, his therapist who helped him reconstruct his own history, claims that Zaretsky remained "acutely aware of what it means to be human." Hope was the other side of Zaretsky's shattered world. He affirmed life *in spite of* the depression that the devastation of his mind caused him. The idea of living kept haunting its opposite:

> Two ideas keep running through my head: I keep telling myself my life is over, that I'm of no use to anyone but will stay this way until I die, which probably won't be long now. On the other hand, something keeps insisting I have to live, that time can heal everything, that maybe all I need is the right medicine and enough time to recover.
> (Luria 1972: 15)

Zaretsky found meaning in musical tunes, even though he could not recognize the words that accompanied them; and he found meaning in nature. Zaretsky also had a purpose: he never gave up writing in spite of the excruciating struggle that it took to produce each word which he could not subsequently recognize. Luria correctly writes that he "remained a man, struggling to regain what he had lost, reconstitute his life, and use the powers he had once had" (Luria 1972: 35). Zaretsky produced meaning by narrating his own tragedy, and he reconstituted it by re-collecting it. As a result, at certain moments he turned his tragic mortality into what I call a near life experience.

I hesitate to mention "hope" until the next chapter, because the word points to something at the other end of a road we have only started to travel, but it helps to know that there is life after the journey through dread that now follows. Zaretsky's narration of being wounded and of the hours and years afterwards evoke more than fear and pity in us. It forces us *to see* mind's inextricable unity with brain in a way that is both unbearable and inescapable.

Russian front, 2 March 1943

Not everyone who is shot in the head survives, and those who do are not always able to reconstruct what happened. Zaretsky is an exception:

> Bullets whistled over my head, I dropped down for cover. But I just couldn't lie there waiting, not while our eagles were starting to climb the bank. Under fire I jumped up from the ice, pushed on . . . toward the west . . . there . . . and . . .
>
> (Luria 1972: 8)

It is astonishing how quickly he later remembers regaining consciousness and of his remembering that he couldn't remember what had happened to him:

> Somewhere not far from our furthest position on the front lines, in a tent blazing with light, I finally came to again . . . . For some reason, I couldn't remember anything, couldn't say anything. My head seemed completely empty, flat, hadn't the suggestion of a thought or memory, just a dull ache and buzz, a dizzy feeling.
>
> (Luria 1972: 8)

Zaretsky vaguely recalls feeling pain for the first time when several people held him down on the operating table so tightly that he couldn't move:

> I was screaming, gasping for breath . . . that warm sticky blood was running down my ears and neck . . . my mouth and lips had a salty taste . . . . I remember that my skull was bursting, and I had a sharp, rending pain in my head . . . . But I had no strength left, couldn't scream any more, just gasped. My breathing stopped – any minute now and I was going to die . . . .
>
> (Luria 1972: 9)

After brain surgery

Recalling the days immediately after the operation, Zaretsky writes:

> My head was a complete blank then. I just slept, woke, but simply couldn't think, concentrate, or remember a thing. My memory – like my life – hardly seemed to exist. At first I couldn't even recognize myself, or what had happened to me, and for a long time (days on end) didn't even know where I'd been hit. My head wound seemed to have transformed me into some terrible baby.
>
> (Luria 1972: 9)

He writes that everything he remembers about the next few months is "scattered" and fragmented into "disconnected bits and pieces," a semi-real existence:

> I'm in a kind of fog all the time, like a heavy half-sleep. My memory's a blank. I can't think of a single word. All that flashes through my mind are some images, hazy visions that suddenly appear and just as suddenly disappear, giving way to fresh images. But I simply can't understand or remember what these mean.
>
> (Luria 1972: 11)

Zaretsky asks,

> Am I dreaming or is this for real? It's lasted too long now to be a dream, that sort of thing doesn't happen, particularly when you know time is passing so quickly. But if this is life, and not a dream, why am I still sick? Why hasn't my head stopped aching and buzzing, why do I always feel so dizzy?
>
> (Luria 1972: 13)

Shattered world

After Zaretsky's bandages were removed, the surface of his head looked as if it had healed, but his world remained fragmented as long as he lived. The shrapnel had permanently shattered his perception, for he lost sight of the right half of everything. When he looked at a book, for instance, he could not see the right page, nor could he see the right side of words on the left page; and when he saw the left half of a word, the right side of every letter vanished. Zaretsky's perception of his own body disintegrated in the same way:

> Once when I left my room and was walking in the corridor, I'd no sooner taken a few steps than I suddenly banged my right shoulder

and the right side of my forehead against the wall and got a bump on my forehead. I was furious; I simply couldn't understand why I'd suddenly bumped into the wall. I should have seen it. Just then I happened to look down – at the floor and at my feet – and I shuddered. I couldn't see the right side of my body. My hands and feet had disappeared. What could have happened to them?

(Luria 1972: 40)

Zaretsky reports that his injury also destroyed his sense of bodily identity. Sometimes he felt that his head was "the size of a table – every bit as big – while my hands, feet, and torso become very small." At other times he suddenly felt extraordinarily tall but his head "very, very tiny – no bigger than a chicken's head." He also had trouble associating parts of his body with their names: "I know what the word *shoulder* means and that the word forearm is closely related to it . . . . But I always forget where my *forearm* is located" (Luria 1972: 40–3).

The magnitude of Zaretsky's suffering did not keep him from struggling with denial: "I still wasn't willing to believe I'd suffered such a cruel head wound and kept insisting it must be a dream. Time was racing by so quickly, so peculiarly." Nor did his irreversible devastation of his mind prevent despair: "I felt as though I were bewitched, lost in some nightmare world, a vicious circle from which there was no way out, no possibility of waking. Nothing I saw made any sense to me" (Luria 1972: 15–16).

Odd self-reference

Our peculiar feelings about Zaretsky's tragedy come from the kind of wound he suffered. If he had been wounded elsewhere besides in the head, our compassion would have a different character. He was wounded in the soul. Dualists escape this by locating the soul elsewhere. The brain's extreme vulnerability might be a source of even more kinds of denial.

Do our brains function in a way that makes them not want to come to terms with themselves? Could it help account for the behaviorist claim that the brain is a "black box"? Might the brain's preoccupation with itself and its denial of itself possibly have the same root? What makes this odd self-reference odd? More questions follow.

Fancies and fears

Warren Gorman suggests that the brain's encasement creates a self-perceptive void. We are not aware of the workings of perception in the same way we are of our heartbeat. We cannot picture brain function in the way we do heart or liver function, according to Gorman. "But while the hand's appendages, the fingers, enable us to feel the hand, and the eye may see itself, one's own brain has not been touched, nor has it been felt, even by the most curious," he notes, then continues by pointing out that "Not only are we denied the possibility of touching our own brains, but also the brain itself is imperceptive to touch." That conflicts with the way in which we perceive the outside of our heads, since "vision constantly informs us of the presence of the head, and that touch and other senses give us many stimuli that arise from the head." By contrast, the organ of perception within is a "perceptive void." As a result, our image of the brain is not "formed by the interaction of perception with conception," as are our images of other parts of the body. This might partly explain why our attitude towards the brain is "rightly overlain with our fancies and our fears" (Gorman 1960: 249–50).

Self-regulation paradox

The brain is responsible for all mental processes, including its regulation of itself. This tempts us to ask if its regulation includes concealing from itself the fact that it is the regulator. G.E. Schwartz uses the term "self-regulation paradox" when he asks "why is it that the brain has no direct experience of the fact that it is actually responsible for all this?" We experience perception and motor activity *"away* from our brain" even though they are "actually constructed out of patterns of subcortical and cortical processes located within the skull" (Schwartz 1980: vii–viii). Does this suggest that the organ of regulation functions in a way that predisposes it not to recognize its function?

Strange recursion

A recursive system "computes that it is computing" so that the "experience experiences itself," according to William Powers. Our point of view about the brain seems to be a strange kind of recursion, as his "gray blob" model implies:

> The nervous system of naive perception is a gray blob, which under a microscope becomes a mass of separate blobs and filaments. We see no organization there; we imagine it .... Somewhere in that gray blob, we must conclude, is the mental model of the gray blob .... This bothers me. Something has been left unsaid, or unthought, or unnoticed. I think the problem lies ... in a certain attitude toward models, one that encourages us to follow our own logic once around the loop and then forget to follow it around again.
>
> (Powers 1980: 240)

Does this suggest that something intrinsically blocks the brain's attempts to be recursive about itself as a bodily organ?

Three dreadful possibilities

The desire that some, fortunately few, have to transplant consciousness surgically breaks the metaphorical bubble in some unusually anxiety-provoking ways.

Brain transplantation

Fetal tissue has been transplanted into adult brains to treat Parkinson's disease. This does not transplant consciousness, but some fantasize about attempting to do so by taking brain material from one person and transplanting it into the brain of another. Speculation about this ranges from using a single cell and inserting it stereotactically into various larger amounts of brain material up to an entire hemisphere. Thankfully all of this is beyond the limits of existing surgical technology and might never be possible. Even if vascular connections etc. could be made and transplanted adult material survived in the recipient's brain, which is clearly possible, certain natural properties of the human CNS would probably keep it from connecting functionally.

A still more extreme fantasy aims at transplanting the whole brain and self-identity along with it. G.W. Miller, knowing that we lack the ability to connect the spinal cord etc., calls attention to an odd point:

> Should the brain become a transplantable organ, the donor would become the recipient. Should Mr. X die of a condition which apparently had not affected his brain, and this brain were to be transplanted into the vegetable-like body of Mr. Y, then Mr. Y, upon rising to the commands of the new brain, would be Mr. Y in physical appearance only, for his brain, the source of life, thought, movement, and memory, would be Mr. X. Thus, in being the donor of a brain, Mr. X would actually become the recipient of the body of Mr. Y. Hence, in actuality, this would be a body transplant, rather than that of a brain.
>
> (Miller 1971: 13–14)

The most extreme fantasies aim, not at transplanting all or a part of the brain, but at preserving it alive in a vat. This strange concept comes mainly from a thought experiment that philosophers use to try to clarify the nature of consciousness. Daniel Dennett, for instance, tries to put the solipsism question into perspective in this way:

> Suppose evil scientists removed your brain from your body while you

slept, and set it up in a life-support system in a vat. Suppose they then set out to trick you into believing that you were not just a brain in a vat, but still up and about, engaging in a normally embodied round of activities in the real world. This old saw, the brain in the vat, is a favorite thought experiment in the toolkit of many philosophers. It is a modern day version of Descartes' evil demon, an imagined illusionist bent on tricking Descartes about absolutely everything, including his own existence . . . . *Might* you be nothing but a brain in a vat? Might you have *always* been a brain in a vat?

(Dennett 1991: 3)

Even if adult brain tissue transplantation is never possible, the fact that a brain can survive being removed from the skull has unfortunately been proven. Since it cannot continue to function without sensory input, vat fantasies are not much more feasible than whole brain transplants at this time.

Head transplantation

Robert White and V.P. Deminkov, however, have proven that heads with brains in them can be transplanted from one monkey to another. I am unconditionally ethically opposed to the animal experimentation leading up to this discovery and also have reservations that are probably insurmountable about violating the self-identity of human beings by transplanting their heads. Yet it can be done and might happen, even though the result will be a paralyzed patient. Nevertheless, my concerns do not keep me from reporting what I learned.

During a private interview on 5 May 1993, White told me that people are less shocked at the thought of transplanting even whole brains than at the prospect of head transplants. If we were to transplant "only" the brain, an observer might still be able to deny at some level that consciousness is located in brains. Transplanting a head would completely destroy that lingering illusion in the most shocking possible way. Denial would break down completely, White says, because the observer would see that consciousness is located in the brain by the response of the head to which it belongs.

Dr White, a most gracious host and manifestly conscientious neurosurgeon, discussed all of this and more during lunch. He said that surgical technology might succeed in spinal cord repair in 50–100 years, which would make human head transplants, or "body transplants" as he calls them, feasible. Learning the extent of ongoing research in how to reconnect severed spinal cords encouraged me, in spite of my dread that someday it might be used to make human head transplantation acceptable.

Brain in a vat

An even more bizarre question came to me after Dr White and I parted. Since a brain can live outside the skull, could it live in a vat artificially connected to a blood supply and sensory input? Technological advances seemed to give a small measure of dreadful credence to this possibility. Science fiction, like Curt Siodmak's novel, *Donovan's Brain* (1942), has kept this dreadful fantasy alive, and so has C.S. Lewis' *That Hideous Strength* (1965), a novel in which the devil takes over a head in a vat experiment. Dan's disturbing dream expresses a similar dread.

Epilogue: the nightmare of Dan

The Lamentation of Dan in "Throwing things" narrates his depression. He already had read my Epilogue just before the second psychizatrist (PZ) pressed him down, trying to cover up the mistake of the first one. During the later stages of treatment by the general practitioner who healed his soul chemically, Dan ran across Dennett's suggestion that a brain in a vat is "a modern day version of Descartes." Then he had a nightmare, while still taking Prozac, that happens to shed new light on the bizarre vat fantasy. The truth of the myth in Dan's nightmare goes beyond the chemical that triggered it. Causes never completely explain products.

Dan dreamed, contrary to reality, that he went to a third PZ, and that this one countered his lament against the first two by actually removing his brain and setting it up in a vat. At this point, Dan's vat dream departs completely from Dennett's version of it. The nightmare PZ did not feed deceptive sensory input into Dan's brain, but plugged the output of a television camera into it instead. The camera showed Dan his actual brain in a vat together with the support systems sustaining it. Seeing his brain see itself did not terrify him, Dan said, but it turned his reflection on himself into an "infinite regression." This absurdity "relativized" even the diabolical sign that the PZ wrote in blood and located visibly above the vat: "This is your brain in a vat. Psychiatrists never make mistakes." This inventive PZ made no mistake about neglecting auditory input torture. He forced Dan's brain to listen to an endless loop tape recording of the actual verbal swill of the previous PZ: "What's love? It's nothing but a man's illusion that one woman is different from other women."

Dan attributes his recovery to this dream, because it objectified and set out in the open what had actually happened to him. Dan laughed after he told me his nightmare and said "Now I know what bad infinity is, and two kinds of it are my dream. My brain invented the hall of mirrors, but the PZs themselves caused the endless auditory loop."

Part five

Light at midnight

The two preceding chapters provoke a peculiar sense of despair in those who have the kind of sensitivity that allows them to hear what they are really saying. The mortality of the human brain and its extreme fragility during life are shorthand statements of the human predicament as such written in large letters. Witnessing the persecution of the organ of consciousness opens the wounds of negativity of life in general in an unusually radical way. Knowing that various kinds of projectiles can penetrate brains, encountering Zaretsky's tragedy, and thinking of the dreadful possibilities torment the rhythm and harmony of consciousness. Compulsion consumes purpose and strange recursion overcomes meaning.

The wounds of life's negativity can be healed only as aesthetic phenomena. Aesthetic healing does not pretend that the wounds do not exist or that it can ever completely close them. It creates a new quality out of chaos by rebinding shreds of meaning and purpose into new rhythms and harmonies. Just as the brain becomes conscious through a certain kind of qualitative leap, even so the healing quality born from the wounds of negativity is another kind of leap. Just as consciousness seems to require self-referent biological processes, aesthetic healing is completed self-reference. It is the true infinity of a loop that fulfills itself, which G.W.F. Hegel also calls "spirit," not the bad infinity of the endlessly repetitive loop in Dan's nightmare.

Hegel observes that a new quality *is* only in conflict with its opposite, a process born out of torment. He illustrates this abysmal truth by playing with the words *quale* (Latin "kind") and *Qual* (German "torment"):

> '*Qualierung*' or '*Inqualierung*', an expression of Jacob Boehme's, whose philosophy goes deep, but into a turbid depth, signifies the movement of a quality . . . within itself in so far as it posits and establishes itself in its negative nature (in its '*Qual*,' or torment) from out of an other – signifies in general the quality's own internal unrest by which it produces and maintains itself only in conflict.
>
> (Hegel 1969 [1816]: 114)

Chapter 9 shows that the fine arts establish the new quality in visual and auditory symbols. Aesthetic apprehension heals negativity by recasting reality as art and defiantly acting *as if* the transfigured product had more validity than the material it uses. Chapter 10 argues that religious faith heals negativity *only if* it keeps a certain kind of aesthetic symbol in a particular way. Chapter 11 argues that the essential foundation of ethics does not depend upon religion. *Even if* religious faith and all metaphysical values are illusions, the valuer is valuable. Each of the three kinds of healing is courageous in its own way. Yet all courage has an aesthetic core, and we have to use aesthetic judgment to detect or produce *meaning* as such. Religious symbols and ethical norms are meaningful because they have aesthetic characteristics. Courage heals by defying the tyranny of despair. It is, to borrow Hegel's words, the "negative of the negative" (Hegel 1969 [1816]: 115).

Chapter 9

Near life experiences[1]

The gods pressed Sisyphus down by condemning him to the most absurd of all possible punishments. They made him roll a stone to the top of a hill; and once he had done this, an unseen sinister force would make it roll to the bottom again. Then he had to roll it to the top once more and so on. The whole meaningless procedure would be repeated for all eternity.

Some consider the fate of Sisyphus more dreadful than that of Ixion, who had to roll in a wheel forever, or the punishment of Tantalus, whose chin was in water, but who could never quench his thirst because the water would always recede when he tried to drink. His fate was perhaps more dreadful than that of Prometheus, who was chained to a rock while an eagle pecked at his liver forever. Sisyphus was condemned to the despair of meaninglessness, the ultimate bad infinity.

Meditation on Sisyphus

Ancient materialist Lucretius knows that this myth is a true statement of the human condition: "*As for all those torments that are said to take place in the depths of Hell, they are actually present here and now, in our own lives.*" The truth of myth goes beyond the fact that it is not to be taken literally:

> Sisyphus . . . is alive for all to see . . . embittered by perpetual defeat. To strive for this profitless and never-granted prize, and in striving toil and moil incessantly, this truly is to push a boulder laboriously up a steep hill, only to see it, once the top is reached, rolling and bounding down again to the flat levels of the plain.
>
> (Lucretius 1932 [c.54 BC]: 117)

The absurd

Albert Camus' *Myth of Sisyphus* says something similar in our time:

> Myths are made for the imagination to breathe life into them. As for

this myth, one sees merely the whole effort of a body straining to raise the huge stone, to roll it and push it up a slope a hundred times over; one sees the face screwed up, the cheek tight against the stone, the shoulder bracing the clay-covered mass, the foot wedging it, the fresh start with arms outstretched, the wholly human security of two earth-clotted hands.

(Camus 1955 [1942]: 89)

Sisyphus' fate is tragic only at certain limited moments when he becomes *"conscious"* during his return to the plain:

I see that man going back down with a heavy yet measured step toward the torment of which he will never know the end. That hour like a breathing-space which returns as surely as his suffering, that is the hour of consciousness.

(Camus 1955 [1942]: 89)

Most of the time, Sisyphus' condition and ours are absurd, according to Camus, for we are "deprived of the memory of a lost home or the hope of a promised land." The absurd is this "divorce between man and his life, the actor and his setting," the collapse of the "stage sets" in our repetitive and futile struggle with time. The absurd is the "nausea" of the "incalcul- able tumble before the image of what we are," our endlessly frustrated "appetite for the absolute," an insatiable "nostalgia for unity." Sisyphus' fate is our "confrontation between the human need and the unreasonable silence of the world." It is the "denseness and that strangeness of the world," and the fact that "Forever I shall be a stranger to myself." The inescapability of the absurd drives Camus to confess that "There is but one truly serious philosophical problem, and that is suicide" (Camus 1955 [1942]: 3).

Happiness

Camus answers "no" to the suicide question because "some profound and constant thought" can "infuse its strength" into our existence: "There is thus a metaphysical honor in enduring the world's absurdity" (Camus 1955 [1942]: 69). Nothing matters in the absurd, and yet life must be lived anyway, according to Camus. That is the cruel logic of the absurd. If he is right, the absurd denies us the option of suicide, for a part of the absurd is the meaningless perpetuation itself. The result, however, is happiness:

One does not discover the absurd without being tempted to write a manual of happiness . . . . Happiness and the absurd are two sons of the same earth. They are inseparable . . . . The struggle itself toward the heights is enough to fill a man's heart. One must imagine Sisyphus happy.

(Camus 1955 [1942]: 90–91)

Aesthetics is the clue to happiness in an absurd existence. Art alone has power to infuse such strength into it: "In this regard the absurd joy par excellence is creation. 'Art and nothing but art,' said Nietzsche, 'we have art in order not to die of the truth.'" In a moment I am going to recollect some of the history of aesthetic affirmation that breathes life into Nietzsche's statement so that we won't trim the surface off what Camus drew from him:

> In this universe the work of art is the sole chance of keeping his consciousness and of fixing its adventures . . . . Explanation is useless, but the sensation remains and, with it, the constant attractions of a universe inexhaustible in quantity. The place of the work of art can be understood at this point.
>
> (Camus 1955 [1942]: 69–70)

Camus believes that the art work has validity even though it is finite and impermanent:

> To work and create "for nothing," to sculpture in clay, to know that one's creation has no future, to see one's work destroyed in a day while being aware that fundamentally this has no more importance than building for centuries – this is the difficult wisdom that absurd thought sanctions. Performing the two tasks simultaneously, negating on the one hand and magnifying on the other, is the way open to the absurd creator. He must give the void its colors.
>
> (Camus 1955 [1942]: 84)

Wrestling with meaninglessness

It is meaningful to wrestle with meaninglessness, the more general name of the human condition that the absurd crowns. To wrestle with it is to care, and to care is to affirm life. Refusing to give in to meaninglessness requires us to go beyond it, get on top of it, and struggle with it courageously.

What kind of courage could possibly wrestle with meaninglessness and prevail? Before answering, remember that the surface is never enough. Meaninglessness is not simply mundane; it is also cosmic. Think about the facts of the cosmos and picture how precariously our absurd strangeness to ourselves and the unreasonable silence of the world are staged on fragile earth. Step back and watch our planet orbit an obscure star in an insignificant part of the cosmos. Stand in that theater and identify the courage that can give color to its void.

Would I be brave if I buried my head in the sands of denial? Or if puffed my ego up to infinity, would that be nobler? Does insensitive bravado master interstellar space? Are anti-taste, power worship, and cruelty manly? The truth is that cruelty, denial, and the other modes of cowardice between them either capitulate to the absurd or excuse it. None of them wrestles with it. They are crutches used to swagger in the fields of impotent pretending. Radical courage *redeems*. It does not pretend. Nor does it whistle in the dark that the absurd does not exist.

The aesthetic as if

The aesthetic act that colors the void *in spite of* meaninglessness transfigures reality by recasting experience and acting *as if* the product has more validity than the material it uses.

Beyond silly madness

Acting that way naturally conflicts with conventional "sanity." An admittedly narrow, but ruggedly hewn and infinitely deep gulf marks the difference between this aesthetic way of standing outside oneself and madness. As Plato's *Phaedrus* explains, the "divine madness" (*enthousiasmos*) "of which the Muses are the source" is more beneficial than conventional ("man-made sanity") madness:

> [T]he greatest blessings come by way of madness, indeed of madness that is heaven sent . . . . This seizes a tender, virgin soul and stimulates it to rapt passionate expression, especially in lyric poetry, glorifying the countless mighty deeds of ancient times for the instruction of posterity. But if any man come to the gates of poetry without the madness of the Muses, persuaded that skill alone will make him a good poet, then shall he and his works of sanity with him be brought to naught by the poetry of madness, and behold, their place is nowhere to be found . . . this sort of madness is a gift of the gods . . . . And our proof assuredly will prevail with the wise, though not with the learned.
>
> (Plato 1972: 244A, 245A–C)

The gulf that divides the kind of madness that Plato says is "heaven sent" from the conventional sort is absolute. These two kinds of "madness" react to the absurd in two different ways. One way is cynical, the other poetic. Cynics perform nihilistic acts of varying degrees of violence like punching little holes in sinking lifeboats. Real poets accept the nude truth of sharks and still turn despair into its musical opposite. Instead of punching holes in the boat, poets already understand more of the depths than either the cynics or the other passengers. "What is a poet?," Kierkegaard asks: "An unhappy man who in his heart harbors a deep anguish, but whose lips are so fashioned that the moans and cries which pass over them are transformed into ravishing music" (Kierkegaard 1959 [1843]: 19). All sinking lifeboats need at least one such poet on board. Courage comes from the music of these poets.

Zaretsky and Orpheus

A.R. Luria reports that Zaretsky found meaning in musical tunes, even though the words accompanying them were fragmented. Harmony and rhythm are what we might call an "alphabet of meaning," quite apart from the words. He recognizes meaning at this level: "I have the same problem with the words of a song as I do with conversation. But I can grasp the melody automatically, just as I was able to recite the alphabet automatically before I learned to recognize letters" (Luria 1972: 155).

Ovid tells how, when Orpheus went to Hades to seek the soul of his wife Eurydice, the music he sang and played temporarily suspended the punishments of the damned:

> As he spoke thus, accompanying his words with the music of his lyre, the bloodless spirits wept; Tantalus did not catch at the fleeting wave; Ixion's wheel stopped in wonder; the vultures did not peck at the liver [of Tityus]; the Belides rested from their urns, and thou, O Sisyphus, didst sit upon thy stone. Then . . . conquered by the song, the cheeks of the Eumenides were wet with tears; nor could the queen nor he who rules the lower world refuse the suppliant. They called Eurydice.
>
> (Ovid 1976 [c.8]: 67)

Out of the spirit of music

The gods called Eurydice and gave her back to Orpheus not mainly on account of the words that accompanied his music, but because the rhythm and harmony were sublime.

I argue that all the fine arts narrate themselves through certain kinds of rhythm and harmony proper to each. Rhythm and harmony are not limited to beat and pitch. Even the art of living makes life worth living through sequence and structure. Plato's *Republic* points out that music consists of words, harmony, and rhythm, and suggests that the last two are basic because they lay hold of even deeper recesses of the soul than words can. I argue that the words of music derive their power second hand from the rhythm and harmony of what they narrate.

Music is rhythm and harmony on their own without further qualification, their source and ground. In the Epilogue I confess my youthful aesthetic conversion. When I heard the music of Bach for the first time, I saw rhythm and harmony in the way in which one "sees" the plot of a mammoth narrative play work itself out and hold together while doing so.

Nietzsche confesses in the *Birth of Tragedy Out of the Spirit of Music* that "It is only as an *aesthetic phenomenon* that existence and history are eternally justified" (Nietzsche 1967 [1872]: 52). The tragic poetry of Aeschylus justifies existence because of the musical power of the spectacle of the suffering of Dionysus. This is what one could call the blood and guts of every primal aesthetic experience. Music is the clue to aesthetics, just as aesthetics is the clue to meaning as such. Nietzsche's manifesto speaks for the human species; he attests to what the main stream of human wisdom has always known about art. Camus, who echoes Nietzsche, seems to extend the aesthetic justification of existence to the art of *living* when he suggests that Sisyphus' struggle fulfills him and that he is happy. Plato's philosophy contains strong Dionysian elements, despite Nietzsche's failure to appreciate them. Raphael Demos correctly notes that even though we split reason and emotion apart, "Plato does not. Reason is not merely detached understanding; it is conviction, fired with enthusiasm" (Demos 1937: 9).

The beneficial power of poetry extends beyond what we normally call the fine arts. He reports that Diotima, legendary priestess who taught Socrates to make love, claims that the creative process as such is poetry: "All creation or passage of non-being into being is poetry or making, and the processes of all art are creative, and the masters of arts are all poets or makers" (Plato 1892: 205B–C). Poetry exemplifies what ought to inspire living, creating, and indeed every narrative play. All of these arts have plots. Aristotle writes: "It is clear, then, from what we have said that the poet must be a 'maker' not of verses but of stories, since he is a poet in virtue of his 'representation,' and what he represents is action" (Aristotle 1965: 1451B, 9). I argue that plot is essentially musical because it is made up of the rhythm and harmony of events.

Alan Bloom also argues that poetry is essentially musical: "Music is the soul's primitive and primary speech," he writes. "Even when articulate speech is added, it is utterly subordinate to and determined by the music and the passions it expresses . . . . Out of the music emerge the gods that suit it, and they educate men by their example and their commandments" (Bloom 1988: 71–2). I conclude that the aesthetic *as if* is always music regardless of which art expresses it. The graphic arts have rhythmic and harmonic architectural characteristics.

Theory as music

Theater and theory are closely related activities that point to what Gustav Mueller calls "the festive beholding of any celebration of life" including tragic plays and the "thinking penetration of life." Mueller asks us to

> Consider the statement so often repeated, 'This sounds good in theory, but is not good practice.' And how full of life, how actual is the original *theoria*. Originally a *theoretikos* was the official ambassador representing his city at the Greek national games or at the oracle of the gods. Later *theoria* was the festive beholding of any celebration of life as a partly divine, partly human spectacle. For Plato, *theoria* is the thinking penetration of life, the vision of the one in the many. For him as well as for Aristotle, it is the highest and most human function of life, an activity that has its own end and its own satisfaction in itself; it is the life of the universe in a loving human conception; theoretical life is the closest imitation of the blessed god, who sees outside of himself as a perfected work what lives in himself and in his mind.
>
> (Mueller 1944: 31–32)

I argue that our beholding and communication of any such spectacle depend upon a rhythmically and harmoniously ordered arrangement of parts. Isn't the order that arranges the parts of theory like architecture, except that it articulates itself through movement? Could we call the rhythms and harmonies of theories unfrozen architecture? Theorizing lets us "see" musical architectonic structures. All theory, as Mueller uses the term, is musical in this sense.

Philosophy as music

Philosophy stages theories for reflection and analysis through the *play* and interplay of ideas, mental images we see (*idein*), even though we do not perceive them with our eyes. Mental images, the ability to see form (*eidos*), have a neurobiological base, as the research of W. Uttal (1988) and others shows. Intuitions of the architectonic of theories, philosophical ideas, and the images associated with auditory musical rhythm and harmony all seem to have something in common that can be stated physically. This suggests that what we can potentially learn about them might not be as arbitrary as positivists think. The musical nature of philosophy is not merely its ideas, but also the rhythm and harmony that structure a theory into an architectonic systematic whole.

Philosophy has other purposes besides being musical. For instance, the logical and scientific analysis of language and materialist systems that shun metaphysics are *also* philosophy. The truth of philosophy is the whole of which all conflicting systems are parts. One such part of philosophy is its musical view of itself. Respect for the truth of the whole does not permit that view of philosophy to rule out the validity of other parts. Nor does it permit any of the other parts to rule out its validity either. Any kind of small-minded intellectual provincialism, regardless of the shape it takes, is insufferable.

Socrates holds a musical view of philosophy while also going beyond it. He thinks philosophy purifies the soul and prepares it for what hopefully lies beyond death, and yet philosophy performs that preparation in *this* life. Philosophy has the power to purify because it "sees" and loves the good, the fair, and the just. Our "sight" of these forms or ideas is fragmentary, and yet our love of them is what purifies us, not because we possess them but because it is ultimately important to pursue them. We do not possess wisdom, but only strive after it, as Pythagoras knew when he called himself a lover, not a possessor, of wisdom.

Philosophical music is an extreme expression of the aesthetic "as if." We could call it metaphysical spite. We cannot know a philosophical system by one of its parts in isolation from the whole, any more than we can identify a musical theme from a single note or chord. Each part of these draws its individual meaning from the whole to which it belongs. Relevance is retrospective and post-destined. You have to hear a theme as a whole in order to "see" it, and it isn't a whole until *play* stretches it to a certain magnitude. How untrendy and scandalous it would be to stretch Plato's dominant theme out and *play* it. After all, it doesn't sound like anything on the current hit parade. Yet hope shrivels when the sublime themes that musically justify existence can no longer be heard and seen. Great events and mighty architectural structures inspire hope.

Neurobiology of rhythm and harmony

Juan Roederer writes that "music seems to be recognized by our brain as the representation of integral, holistic auditory images (the harmonic structure), whose (long-term) success in time bears in itself a holistic Gestalt value (the melodic contours)" (Roederer 1982: 45).

The two hemispheres seem to have different musical roles, since the right is holistic and intuitive while the left is analytic and sequential, according to Roederer. The left hemisphere seems to be the main source of rhythm because the same sequencer that makes language possible produces it as well. More recent research suggests that both hemispheres have cellular circuits that recognize both language and music, while the left has some regions that recognize only language and the right some that specialize only in music.

Harmony

Hans M. Borchgrevink attributes pitch and tonality to the right hemisphere, while Scott Makeig hypothesizes that both hemispheres are involved in the recognition of pitch: "*Interval quality* (and timbre) might be better perceived using the *right hemisphere*, whereas rapid and accurate *pitch-trajectory* tracking might be better performed using the *left hemisphere*" (Makeig 1982: 232). The visual images associated with music also seem to be closely linked to the brain's perception of harmony.

Images and harmony are "referential," according to Carl Pribram. Reference is correlation "between input and output, between sender and receiver" and provides information by relating "indicant and symbol to the sensory input through which they derive," according to Pribram. He claims that reference depends upon *semantic processing*,

> which relates indicant and symbol to the sensory input from which they derive, is carried out by systems which involve the posterior cortical convexity of the brain, especially in the intrinsic "association" areas that surround the cortex which initially receives the input (the primary sensory projection areas).
>
> (Pribram 1982: 24)

The same posterior cortical systems that help to produce images also "reduce redundancy," not by deleting information, but by correlating it "much as an editor searching for novelty" (Pribram 1982: 29).

Meaning as such is not referential in Pribram's view. He thinks that meaning and reference are based on separate neurobiological processes. He thinks that true musical meaning depends upon a non-referential type of processing which he attributes to rhythm.

Rhythm

Manfred Clynes and Janice Walker characterize rhythm as "reiteration – in space, or in time, or in both" (Clynes and Walker 1982: 171). The non-referential quality of rhythm might be the source of musical meaning. Pribram notes Leonard Bernstein's comment that "music has intrinsic meanings of its own which are not to be confused with specific feelings or moods, and certainly not with pictorial expressions or stories." Following this suggestion, Pribram writes that such meanings are "derived from the intrinsic organization of the music, its structure" which "intends and evokes feelings rather than referencing them" (Pribram 1982: 28).

Musical meaning is a type of repetition that depends upon *pragmatic processing*, which, according to Pribram, relates sign and symbol to their user [and] is carried out by systems which involve the frontolimbic cortical formations of the brain. . . . [They] intimately interconnect the core portions of the brain such as the mesencephalic reticular formation and hypothalamus with the frontal lobes of the cerebral cortex.

(Pribram 1982: 24)

These frontolimbic systems also generate and control "feelings produced by repetition" as well as process "variations on repetition, especially temporal variations." Meaning is based on a particular rhythmic quality, namely its *redundancy*. Pribram suggests that "the amygdala of the limbic systems and the related frontal cortex are critically involved in processing redundancy" (Pribram 1982: 27, 29). Meaning differs from information processing, which reduces redundancy. On the contrary, meaning is the redundancy of

> innumerable variations on the structure of a theme . . . meanings are conveyed by patterns of repetitions of referents, repetitions of the information to which the elements of the utterances (phonemes, words) refer. The information conveyed by a literary masterpiece may be encapsulated in an abstract or digest – what makes the original exercise a masterpiece is the meaning generated by slight variations on the informative theme, a theme that is perhaps endlessly repeated as in the repetitions of behavior that characterize the tragic hero in Greek drama. The very variations themselves assume some basic repetitive pattern so that variation can be assessed.
>
> (Pribram 1982: 26)

Epilogue: the dancing word

Rhythm contributes to the production of myths and also resolves the problems myths present, according to Eugene d'Aquili. He traces the production of myths especially to the brain's *binary* and *value* cognitive operators. Among other things, the former sets up polar opposites, such as inside–outside and before–after, in such a way that each "derives meaning from contrast with the other pole," while the latter assigns "an affective valence" to those opposites (Chapter 6).

While the content of myths seems to come mainly from the intuitive right hemisphere, the analytic left hemisphere might be responsible for ordering that primitive content into a kind of rhythmic sequence. D'Aquili further hypothesizes that this process "arises, at least partially, from the elaboration of those parts of the brain which generate and moderate rhythmicity in the ritual behavior of lower animals" (d'Aquili 1986: 155). This suggests that a kind of reptilian dance helps form the words that constitute a myth just as it also helps dissolve it. The same dance also seems to be limbic play.

These processes that transform myth suggest that d'Aquili's hypothesis can account for two senses of meaning, neither of which is referential. Meaning is first the endurance of order during transformation: "The very stability of the overall constellation of relationships and of the neural events which generate them is . . . that a given surface manifestation of structure is meaningful. Meaningfulness, therefore, derives from the stability of neural connections" (d'Aquili 1986: 154). Isn't this stability a kind of harmony? The rhythmic dance of rituals seems to have meaning in a still deeper sense because it resolves the problems that the mythical polarities express, as the next chapter explains. D'Aquili thinks a myth's origin is partly rhythmic and its destiny more radically so:

> Humans may use rhymicity as one way powerfully and affectively to resolve the polarities of myth structure . . . . Thus it appears that the word arises from the dance only to use the dance for its incarnation both in psyche and in society . . . . The dance has formed the word and the word the myth which has guided the dance to an awareness of itself.
>
> (d'Aquili 1986: 155, 160)

Chapter 10

God and evil [1]

Religious faith exists *only if* [2] believers attribute ultimate importance to the narratives they keep. At the same time, narratives must merit having that kind of importance attributed to them. A narrative can redeem *only if* its plot has sublime magnitude. This magnitude is not quantitative. Plots are not extended in space like graphic art, which is normally immobile. Like all the arts of movement, plots exist in time; they are sequences of symbols bound together into a meaningful whole. Sublime magnitude of plot is clearly not infinite extension in time, but the rhythm and harmony of narrative parts deployed within a finite beginning, middle, and end.

Religious narratives must have a cosmological view of "reality as a systematic, multicameral, dynamic, and organic whole," wrestle with its possible "eschatological demise," be able to express what their symbols mean through myth and poetry, and interpret experience in the light of those symbols. Ritual must recollect and verify them by transforming them into "direct experience," thereby completing the "cycle of meaning" that makes the narrative "fully 'religious' in the literal Latin sense of *religare*, 'to rebind'" (Laughlin, McManus, and d'Aquili 1992: 214, 228).

Radical faith

The "rebinding" process that follows begins on the far side of where the atheism of Albert Camus leaves off. The kind of faith it affirms actually depends upon a type of courage that comes to life only after the collapse of less radical types of theism, as Paul Tillich suggests: *The courage to be is rooted in the God who appears when God has disappeared in the anxiety of doubt"* (Tillich 1952: 152).

Radical faith holds real doubt fast by calling the meaning of everything into question, yet affirms life in spite of doubt. Theoretical arguments fail to prove that God exists, as Immanuel Kant knows. Faith does not renounce reason or passively acquiesce to an external rule or potentate. On the contrary, it safeguards the rhythms and harmonies of the symbols that constitute it. I argue that religious symbols are a species of aesthetics, and faith is the kind of pragmatic posture that stakes belief on them.

Socrates finds it worthwhile "to stake everything" on his hope of surviving death. Kant postulates the existence of God, and Søren Kierkegaard, following him, views religious faith as a unique act of the will. Some who have not struggled through Kierkegaard's own words call him "irrational." Far from that, he recognizes, as Kant does, that theoretical reason cannot prove that God exists, and his faith actually *requires* doubt: He writes that "*An objective uncertainty, held fast through appropriation with the most passionate inwardness, is the truth*, the highest truth there is for an *existing* person" (Kierkegaard 1992 [1846]: 203). Faith is risk. It contradicts objective uncertainty:

> If I am able to apprehend God objectively, I do not have faith; but because I cannot do this, I must have faith. If I want to keep myself in faith, I must continually see to it that I hold fast the objective uncertainty, see to it that in the objective uncertainty I am "out on 70,000 fathoms of water" and still have faith.
>
> (Kierkegaard 1992 [1846]: 204)

The most serious defect of Kierkegaard's theism is its failure to grasp the aesthetic dimension of biblical faith, even though he (or one of his pseudonyms) understands the redemptive power of art when he describes a poet as transforming "moans and cries" into "ravishing music" (Kierkegaard 1959 [1843]: 19). Friedrich Nietzsche's affirmation of the justification of "existence and history" as an "*aesthetic phenomenon*" (Nietzsche 1967 [1872]: 52) reveals what Kierkegaard's blind spot keeps him from seeing. The fact that Nietzsche casts this intuition in an increasingly atheistic mode does not keep it from resolving the practical problem of evil either within biblical faith or outside it, as I explain below.

Religion is a species of the aesthetic "as if." Therefore faith does not conflict with science. Such conflict exists in the popular mind, but not in reality, as Kant, the most enlightened philosopher of the Enlightenment, shows in the *Critique of Judgement*. This decisive statement of Kant's aesthetic philosophy (which inspires Nietzsche) reconciles the supposed conflict between science and religion because it reconciles the difference between scientific *schemata* and aesthetic *symbols*, since (as Chapter 1 indicates) "all our knowledge of God is merely symbolical" (Kant 1968 [1790]: Sec. 59).

The best side of Kierkegaard's theism (despite his oblivion to Kant's aesthetic philosophy) is his grasp of Kant's practical postulation of faith. He recognizes that faith is largely an act of the will in which "the individual relates himself to a something in such a way that his relation is in truth a God-relation" (Kierkegaard 1992 [1843]: 199). Faith rebinds in

Kiekegaard's terms through the courage of the passionate inwardness that comes from holding fast the objective uncertainty. The faith that begins on the nether side of profound atheism negates negativity by including both Nietzsche's aesthetic justification and Kierkegaard's subjective certainty.

Two problems of evil

The bomb that destroyed the federal building in Oklahoma City on 19 April 1995 also damaged St Paul's Episcopal Cathedral a few blocks away. Dean George Back describes what happened:

> What was that? Those shocked first minutes. Not here! It must have been gas. It could not be intentional. And then a dreadful confirmation, crowds running up the street, men in FBI jackets yelling, "Evacuate, evacuate!" another device is feared.
>
> There is a huge mob outside St. Anthony's Hospital. There is not space in the building to gather the medical volunteers. Inside people stream through the crowded halls like cells through a vein. Clergy gather with family members of victims in the gymnasium.
>
> Out of ten thousand dark, distant, terrible fantasies, one has exploded in our face. Like an ancient giant beast it mangles and devours our children. We should have known, should have suspected, should have been paranoid about the hostility rampant in our world.
>
> The monster's breath dissolves concrete into chunks of dust, and now we search for life among the rocks. The monster multiplies itself into a billion glass claws, and now we sew together torn flesh. The monster emerges from some sewer of toxic hatred and now we seek to trace the pollution to some source.
>
> Our old Cathedral lies struck. Five of the six dormers have fallen. The bricks and stones crushing the bushes and benches beneath them. The St. Francis window lies crumbled and twisted amidst the pews. It's companion dangles among the organ trumpet pipes. The roof has shifted. Shafts of daylight come through and you can see the dust hover in the air. The heavy oak doors are ten feet into the cloister. The new front doors hold, but the casings pop out of the wall on the inside.
>
> A few hundred feet away, behind barricades, emergency vehicles and police lines, worse things are being revealed. In numerous places the damage is to human life. The child care center is decimated. The reports of the workers bring horror and anger and tears.
>
> (Back 1995: 1).

Multiply this picture by all the innocent suffering that has ever occurred and all that ever will, and it creates supreme uncertainty about God's existence. Alternatively, take even the smallest fragment of the evil that happened at Oklahoma City, Hiroshima, or wherever and whenever the innocent have suffered, and the result is the same. There are actually two problems of evil. The first looks toward the past and asks what the *origin* of evil is. The second momentarily suspends that question and turns its attention to the *destiny* of evil; it asks how evil can be overcome or transfigured now and in the future.

The origin of evil

The biblical problem of evil, stated more fully, comes to this: A person who believes in God must make three fundamental claims at the same time, and yet it is impossible to make all of them: (1) Evil is a true fact of human experience. (2) God is good. (3) God is omnipotent. That is the problem in all its well-known horrible simplicity. Theists can logically make any two, but not all three, of the foregoing statements, and they have used thousands of gallons of ink to write their way out of the problem only to find that they have inked themselves into a corner. The problem of evil is the atheist's strongest argument against belief in God. Shallow atheism scoffs at symbols of God because they do not fit petty materialisms like crude capitalism, crude communism, and other small materialist ideologies. Real atheism, by contrast, apprehends what the symbols of God mean enough to conclude that his existence is impossible in the face of the problem of innocent suffering, for it opens an abyss of unquenchable doubt.

The problem of the origin of evil, viewed historically, is the product of the kind of theism that negates the wickedness of the gods. The biblical and Platonic theologies both insist that God is good. We learn in the *Republic* that "the god and what belongs to the god are in every way in the best condition" (Plato 1968: 381B). This theory creates a problem of evil. Since the god does not cause evil, what does?

Biblical religion has an even more acute problem of evil because it, unlike the Platonic system, attributes omnipotence to the creator and thereby produces unquenchable doubt. The end of this chapter qualifies the theoretical doubt *theoretically* by calling the popular version of omnipotence into question. This changed conceptual perspective, however, does not pretend to quench the doubt of those who *actually* suffer innocently. That doubt is the core "objective uncertainty" that radical faith holds fast at all times and upon which it depends. Biblical and Platonic theism both have to ask: *How can evil arise in a good cosmos?*

Biblical negation

The biblical affirmation that God is good has roots in the Babylonian world-view it tries to overcome. The Babylonian epic (Gaster 1958: 52–70) that expresses this view dates from before 2000 BC. Apsu and Tiamat, primal god and goddess of salt and fresh water, mate by mingling their waters to give birth to subsequent deities, some of which eventually are less chaotic. The appearance of Marduk and other later generation gods challenges Apsu and Tiamat; war then breaks out across the generation gap. As in similar epics, the later "good" gods are partly, but not completely, victorious. The legacy of original evil still haunts the cosmos, since they "create" it out of Tiamat's dead but still evil body. They execute Kingu, her lover and secretary of war, and make human beings out of his body. As Paul Ricoeur notes, here is the perfect doctrine of original sin. This shows that the idea of original sin is also pre-biblical, contrary to what John Durant seems to think (Chapter 2).

How can we account for any human overcoming of evil, if we ourselves are essentially evil? How can we account for the leap from evil to good in Marduk and other gods of his generation? The Babylonian inability to answer this is its version of the problem of good. The two biblical creation narratives, if taken to their logical conclusion, produce the problem of evil by negating the Babylonian view that evil is a part of the original condition of the cosmos. They assert that both God and the created order are good *in spite of* abundant objective uncertainties and innocent suffering that seemed to confirm what they negate.

The first biblical account (Genesis 1:1–2:3) preserves the symbolism of the waters but negates the idea that they are evil by asserting God's sovereignty over them in creating light. The author might have been a Jew exiled *in* Babylon. This account of creation is a unique act of courage, pragmatically significant as a protest in exile, and aesthetically sublime. The second account (Genesis 2:4–25), obviously by a different author, begins with dry dust, not water. It also affirms the goodness of God and, except for the serpent, of the created order. These two narratives force us to try to account for the leap to evil, seeing that both creator and creation are good. Why is this problem so opaque? Paul Ricoeur (1967) thinks that the author of the second narration deliberately preserves the ambiguity that produces the opacity. On the one hand, Adam and his woman, not yet named Eve, who stand for humankind as such, are responsible for evil because they break the bond of trust with the Lord God. On the other hand, they and we are also victims, since the serpent is already evil and tempts them to their fatal decision.

The extreme identification of God as good and the opacity of identifying humankind as simultaneously culprit and victim gives Genesis 3 extraordinary insight into human ambiguity. The deliberate theological inconsistency of keeping an evil monster from the Babylonian scheme sheds light on the human condition. Ricoeur describes the deceptive way in which this particular left-over reptile uses language. He tricks Adam and his woman into disobedience, not through sex as the many may think, but by insinuating uncertainty and ambiguity.

Platonic negation

Plato affirms that the gods are good by trying to overcome the world-views of epic and tragic poetry. He deliberately negates the epic theology that the gods and cosmos were originally evil. He reacts against Hesiod's *Theogony*, the western version of the Babylonian epic. Hesiod differs from his source by postponing the origin of evil somewhat. The first deities that come into being are not manifestly evil, even though Eros, "fairest of the deathless gods," is a troublemaker who "unnerves the limbs and good counsels of men and gods." Evil begins when Uranus has incest with his mother Gaia and murders their children. Chronos the Titan, a child he does not murder, castrates him and temporarily takes over his role as chief deity. Aphrodite comes into being from the foam caused by the severed sex organs of Uranus when they fall into the ocean. She and Eros then take their place together among the blessed gods. Zeus, son of Chronos, overthrows his father, and except for his own private sex life, reigns virtuously. Like Marduk, his Babylonian counterpart, Zeus never completely overcomes the earlier evil. The Titans preserve its legacy, and he constantly struggles against their wickedness. How can we account for the leap from evil to "good" in Zeus and Aphrodite? This epic's inability to answer, like that of its Babylonian source, is the problem of good.

Tragedy is partly rooted in the epic belief that "the divine comes to be through anger and suffering," according to Ricoeur. He thinks that divine malevolence predestines the hero's destruction. The gods cause the fault, *hybris*, or other traits for which they then blame the hero, torture him with what I call "slow hook 'sport'," and finally crush him:

> Tragedy requires, on the one hand, transcendence and, more precisely hostile transcendence – "pitiless god, thy hand alone has guided all," says Racine's Athalia, – and, on the other hand, the upsurge of a freedom that *delays* the fulfillment of fate, causes it to hesitate and to appear contingent at the height of the crisis, in order finally to make it break out in a "dénouement," where its fatal character is ultimately revealed.
>
> (Ricoeur 1967: 220–1)

Ricoeur thinks that this "tragic theology" cannot be stated in words or worked out reflectively but can only be shown dramatically in "the characters in a spectacle, in the vestments of poetry, and through the specific emotions of terror and pity" (Ricoeur 1967: 225).

Plato's negation of divine maleficence in epic and tragic poetry produces a problem of evil similar to, but less acute than, that of the biblical negation. In the *Timaeus*, the Demiurge ("worker for the people") creates the cosmos as nobly as possible by looking to eternal ideas like the just and the fair as his model. His power is limited in the sense that the Receptacle of his creative work already exists, but this feminine material also "somehow partakes of the good." Matter is not evil as some *neo*-Platonists later held.

Even though there might be many causes of evil, the *Republic* claims the God is not one of them:

> "Then," I said "the god, since he's good, wouldn't be the cause of everything, as the many say, but the cause of a few things, for human beings and not responsible for most. For the things that are good for us are far fewer than those that are bad; and of the good things, no one else must be said to be the cause; of the bad things, some other causes must be sought and not the god."
>
> (Plato 1968: 379C)

The *Republic* analyzes one cause of evil, namely human injustice, something human souls do to themselves, with extraordinary clarity, but it cannot adequately explain the other causes. At the same time, his extreme identification of the God with the good also makes Plato extraordinarily clear about who the God is, quite apart from whether or not he exists. Plato's relentless theological consistency defines what the symbol of the God has to be, namely "never departing from his idea," a plenitude of "virtue" and "beauty," as well as "altogether simple and true."

The destiny of evil

The biblical and Platonic negations both hold fast to the divine goodness, and they also seek deliverance from evil through a metaphorical journey. Platonic deliverance looks forward to the soul's journey into a future in which it will once again intuit the ideas in their fullness without needing a body. Biblical deliverance looks forward to the coming of the Kingdom of God and the resurrection of the dead. Hope for beatific outcomes like these redeems by anticipating.

Restoration

In both systems, the journey is a kind of restoration, but not a strange loop that takes us back to where we started. It points to where we have not yet been in a narrative plot that has a beginning, middle, and an end. The end of the journey resembles the beginning more than either does the middle. In the Platonic myth, the soul intuited the ideas of the good, the fair, and the just close to its origins. Its destiny is to intuit them again, but not in exactly the way it originally did, since its experiences here and now add something. Tillich calls this the "new being," namely the good that emerges in the ambiguous struggle with evil between origin and destiny.

In spite of its silence on religion, the triune brain concept suggests what the neurobiological base of redemption symbols might be. James B. Ashbrook, using MacLean's research as his point of departure to explain religious experience as such, argues that the right and left hemispheres of the neocortex produce different kinds of religious ideas. The differences arise partly from the ways in which the two hemispheres are connected with the limbic system. Faith, the "experiential anchoring of what matters most in life," is produced by the old brain's influence on the two neocortical hemispheres. Beliefs involve both hemispheres. The right hemisphere responds to limbic activities that produce conviction (one of MacLean's "gratulant" affects) that beliefs are true and important. The left hemisphere, however, "explains" this subneocortical experience. Faith as such, religious or otherwise, seems to arise, as Ashbrook suggests, from limbic conviction. Religious faith, however, is conviction in regard to certain types of events and symbols.

Redemption symbols might be based on the family-related behavior MacLean traces back to the late subphase of neomammalian evolution. The functions MacLean attributes to the thalamocingulate subphase of limbic evolution might partly explain how the human brain produces an even wider range of religious analogies, according to Ashbrook. These include Tillich's "anxiety of meaninglessness" as a variation on the paleomammalian "separation call" (Ashbrook 1989: 71).

The same paleomammalian responsibility for the young which MacLean thinks helps produce conscience might also generate religious symbols, and the parental rescue of lost offspring might be the neurobiological base of redemption symbols. Creation, fall, and redemption might be analogical modifications of the original unity of the nursing female and her offspring, its disruption, and parental rescue. The lost offspring does not initiate the rescue that leads to the "happy ending" but accepts parental acceptance. Tillich writes that "the act of accepting meaninglessness is in itself a meaningful act" because it is "an act of faith."

Sublime magnitude

Restoration symbols redeem partly on account of their content, but also because they are aesthetic spectacles, just as the music of Orpheus temporarily suspends the punishments of the damned. Nietzsche's aesthetic justification of existence also attests to the nature of redemption. It is the tragic spectacle itself that justifies existence. Ricoeur considers it the essence of tragic deliverance:

> There remains the tragic *spectacle* itself, to purify whoever yields himself to the sublimity of the poetic word . . . an aesthetic transposition of fear and pity by virtue of a tragic myth turned into poetry and by the grace of an ecstasy born of a spectacle.
>
> (Ricoeur 1967: 231)

Even though Plato negates the theological base of tragedy, he also affirms the redemptive power of the spectacle of a sense object that reawakens recollection of the original "vision" of the ideas, for instance in the *Phaedrus*:

> But when one who is fresh from the mystery, and saw much of the vision, beholds a godlike face or bodily form that truly expresses beauty, first there comes upon him a shuddering and a measure of that awe which the vision inspired, and then reverence as at the sight of a god . . . a holy image of deity.
>
> (Plato 1972: 251A)

The Bible is filled with aesthetic spectacles, the burning bush Moses saw and his appearance after descending from Mount Sinai, and the Transfiguration of Christ. Isaiah's vision in the temple is such a spectacle:

> In the year that King Uzziah died I saw also the Lord sitting upon a throne, high and lifted up, and his train filled the temple. Above it stood the seraphims; each one had six wings; with twain he covered his face, and with twain he covered his feet, and with twain he did fly. And one cried to one another and said, Holy, holy, holy, is the Lord of hosts; the whole earth is full of his Glory.
>
> (Isaiah 6:1–3)

This sense of the holy is similar to "weight, grandeur, and energy" of what pagan Longinus calls "transcendent sublimity." He detects the sublime in Genesis: "'God said' – what? 'let there be light,' and there was light. 'Let there be earth,' and there was earth" (Longinus 1965 [*c*.60]: 149). Despite his amusing misquotation, Longinus has inadvertently identified the aesthetic core of religious faith.

The music of Orpheus reveals this core when it temporarily caused the punishments of the damned to cease. As I write elsewhere, "religious symbols gain their validity from their aesthetic power to transfigure suffering" (Casserley 1990: xxiv). How odd it is that Nietzsche's claim about the aesthetic justification of existence ironically helps to explain biblical redemption. Eastern Orthodox theologian and philosopher Nicolas Berdyaev thinks that the gospel brings aesthetic justification. He writes that "Beauty will save the world, i.e. beauty is the salvation of the world. The transfiguration of the world is the attainment of beauty. The kingdom of God is beauty" (Berdyaev 1960 [1931: 247). God's real answer to Job's innocent suffering is the sublime spectacle of his appearance in the whirlwind. Sublime magnitude gives religious symbols their aesthetic power to transfigure suffering.

Religious faith requires a sublimely transcendent plot in order to redeem aesthetically. The magnitude of such a plot is not quantitative endlessness, but completed self-reference of a musical type. Like all significant verbal narratives, a redemptive plot emerges from pre-verbal rhythms and harmonies and resolves itself back into them. Faith is ultimately based less on language than on events that express the "transcendent sublimity" and do not cloy with sentimentality, but confess only robust events devoid of anything small scale and marginal. The rhythm and harmony of redemption that run through the narrative generate a plot with uncanny simplicity and epic brightness.

Longinus inspired a tradition of sensitivity to the sublime that extends through Kant to Rudolf Otto, who describes the "holy" as "inherently 'wholly other'" than ordinary experience. Faith exists only if it has the "awfulness" of the "mysterium tremendum" at its center. Its narrative has to be "uncanny" and overpowering in the massiveness of its plot. This gravity uplifts and does not press down. The sublime "elevates" and is "joyous," according to Longinus, just as Otto claims that the mystery of the holy "captivates and transports" and can fill us with a "strange ravishment." Otto describes the holy ("numinous") as "*mysterium tremendum fascinans*," the pre-ethical sense of the sacred. "*Mysterium tremendum*" is the "awfulness," "overpoweringness," and "energy" (urgency) at the center of the holy. The "awfulness" of that core is "eerie" or "uncanny," not fearful. The mystery of "*mysterium*" is not something inexplicable, but the sublimity that makes the holy "inherently 'wholly other'" than ordinary experience. At the same time, the "*fascinans*" of the holy attracts us and "allures with a potent charm." Otto notes that music expresses the holy in an extraordinarily powerful way:

> Music stands too high for any understanding to reach, and an all-mastering efficacy goes forth from it, of which, however, no man is able to give an account. Religious worship cannot therefore do without music. It is one of the foremost means to work upon men with an effect of marvel.
>
> (Otto 1969 [1917]: 150–1).

Neurobiology of the holy

A number of hypotheses shed light on how the brain might generate the *mysterium tremendum fascinans*. Two are especially pertinent.

MacLean's triune brain concept might inadvertently point to some characteristics of Otto's description of the holy. Certain elements, such as "awfulness," "overpoweringness," and "energy" (urgency), seem to have affinities with MacLean's general limbic affects or variations of them. For instance, "awfulness" ("eerie" or "uncanny") is not fear as such, but possibly a modification of it or some other limbic affect or combination of affects. At the same time, these ways of experiencing the numinous, especially "overpoweringness," might have more primitive neurobiological roots than the limbic system. Furthermore, reptilian "submission" to power might be a source of "absolute dependence." Otto suggests that *"mysterium"* and *"fascinans"* are opposite ways in which we experience the numinous object. The former is the feeling that it is "inherently 'wholly other," the latter attraction to it as "something that allures with a potent charm." This affective ambivalence might be related to the "strangeness" and "familiarity" that MacLean believes are limbic elaborations of protoreptilian dispositions.

Eugene d'Aquili's "aesthetic-religious continuum" is an especially important contribution to the neurobiological study of the holy. He hypothesizes that aesthetic and religious experience have the same neurobiological base. Location on the spectrum "depends on how far tilted it is in the direction of wholeness," a specialized function of the "holistic operator" of the right hemisphere. The more this function exceeds "a state of balance with the analytic functions of the left hemisphere, the stronger will be the associated emotional charge" (d'Aquili 1986: 157). This continuum has four stages.

It begins with "aesthetic perception," which is "a sense of meaning and wholeness which transcends the constituent parts" of the beautiful object "whether a piece of music, a painting, a sculpture, or a sunset," etc. The degree of transcendence at this stage is "slight to moderate." The holy as such ("numinosity"), the next stage on the spectrum, occurs when "the holistic operator functions with a degree of intensity which generates a very marked sense of meaning and wholeness, expanding well beyond the parts perceived, or well beyond the image generated . . . . the connotation of what is perceived vastly exceeds the denotation." Religious myths are both structured and transformed at this stage of the continuum (d'Aquili 1986: 157).

"Cosmic consciousness" or "religious exultation" is the third stage. The holistic operator increasingly overwhelms "synthetic perception," bestowing a sense of meaning and wholeness on all discrete being, both subjective and objective. The essential unity, purposefulness, and goodness of the universe is perceived as a primary datum in spite of knowledge and perception of evil in the world. During this state there is nothing whatever that escapes the mantle of wholeness and purposefulness. This state does not obliterate discrete being, however, and it certainly exists within a temporal matrix. The fourth stage, "absolute unitary being," is "the absolute functioning of the holistic operator" in which "there is nothing but a timeless and perfect sense of meaning and wholeness without any perception of discrete entities" (d'Aquili 1986: 158).

Just as the rhythm of the "dancing word" initially elaborates myths that express the human predicament as antinomies "such as life–death, good–evil, and heaven–hell," the rhythm of ritual also resolves the mythical antinomies, according to d'Aquili. Ceremonial ritual resolves the existential problem at the base of the predicament by unifying the "seemingly irreconcilable opposites which constitute the problem." D'Aquili thinks that rhythm, a left hemisphere activity, can operate independently of the words of prayer that might accompany it and, if "supersaturated" with "*intense firing*," spill over into the right hemisphere, exciting the holistic operator, especially in the fourth stage of the continuum (d'Aquili 1986: 259, 283).

Symbolic activities, including the religious type, are neurobiological processes of brain/mind unities. There is a delicate balance between holding that all mental events are brain events and making the distorted claim that they are nothing but the process that explains their existence. Even though religious ideas are brain events, that fact neither invalidates their meaning nor precludes the possibility that they point to and participate in something beyond the neurobiological processes that bring them to consciousness.

Epilogue: critique of pure power

Radical faith preserves the non-authoritarian authority of ritual spectacle. Liturgy reenacts and anticipates the events in which faith stakes belief as an aesthetically sublime spectacle that justifies existence. Liturgy is untrue to itself when it dries up and capitulates to triviality or sentimentality, since anti-taste is the breeding ground of intolerance.

Authoritarian indoctrination, secular as well as religious, coerces others to submit to beliefs from the outside. This cuts faith off from its source, dries it up, and turns it into rules to which the gullible acquiesce. Contrary to this authoritarianism, liturgy is the primordial aesthetic model of authority. Liturgy is non-authoritarian authority, as Julian Casserley suggests when he writes that

> it is the function of the liturgy to repeat and perpetuate the patterns of the divine redemption which we proclaim in the gospel and expound

in our theology. In this sense the liturgy is obviously the most authoritative element in Christian practice and provides us with the touchstone of authority.

(Casserley 1960: 95)

Similarly doctrines have non-authoritarian authority if we regard them as interpretive categories. Casserley argues thus about "dogmas," religious and otherwise:

> Our dogmas are logical tools of the utmost importance. They are not so much ideas which we question as concepts in terms of which we ask questions. A set of dogmas establish and compose a point of view from which we experience and interpret the world. To us dogma means very much the same thing as presupposition in Collingwood and category in Kant. Of course our dogmas can always be questioned, but that does not prevent them from being presupposed in most of our questions.
>
> (Casserley 1990: 74)

Liturgical spectacle reenacts the central event of its redeeming narrative. Babylonian new year rituals reenacted Marduk's triumph over primal chaos. Every religion has such core symbols. In the case of the Christian religion, these are the death, resurrection, ascension, and second coming of Christ. The most primeval Christian symbol, however, is the Incarnation of Christ, because it contains and summarizes the four redemptive events: "And the Word was made flesh, and dwelt among us, (and we beheld his glory, the glory as of the only begotten of the Father,) full of grace and truth" (John 1:14).

The Incarnation includes creation as well as redemption, since the Word was the means by which God creates: "In the beginning was the Word, and the Word was with God, and the Word was God" (John 1:1). This symbol is anti-gnostic; it means that flesh is essentially good, matter is real and important, and that biological existence is a part of human self-identity. The Incarnation validates our existence by bringing the divine and human natures into a dialectic of difference and identity. Richard Hooker describes this dialectic:

> To gather therefore into one sum all that hitherto hath been spoken touching this point, there are but four things which concur to make complete the whole state of our Lord Jesus Christ: his Deity, his manhood, the conjunction of both, and the distinction of the one from the other being joined in one .... In four words ... *truly, perfectly, indivisibly, distinctly*; the first applied to his being God, and the second to his being Man, the third to his being of both One, and the fourth to

his still continuing in that one Both: we may fully by way of
abridgement comprise whatsoever antiquity hath at large handed . . .
in declaration of Christian belief.

(Hooker 1954 [1549]: 218)

The symbol of the Incarnation is valid, not because church councils
imposed it externally, but because it is the final interpretive category of
everything that liturgy reenacts and anticipates. Furthermore, it strips the
interplay of divine and human difference and identity down to definitive
simplicity. The interplay does not dominate; both natures leave one
another completely intact. The Incarnation reveals a quality that is not
primarily power, namely grace. It elevates human nature and bestows
latitude upon it. By doing so, the symbol of the Incarnation subverts
fixation on pure power as the chief divine attribute. There are only two
reasonable answers to the problem of the origin of evil. One is true atheism, which says that the existence of God is impossible in the face of the
problem of innocent suffering. The other is Plato's answer that the God is
identical with the good and we must seek other causes of evil.

Biblical religion forsakes its own inherent monism when it accepts
Plato's (more likely Descartes') dualistic split between body and soul but
hesitates to accept the Platonic challenge to follow its own belief that God
is good to its relentless conclusion. Ask the question about any case of
innocent suffering: "Why did God let someone bomb the federal building
in Oklahoma City?" Plato answers "He didn't." Like all "conclusions"
about the problems of evil and good, this one leaves much that is opaque,
but it reaffirms what matters most, namely that God never causes and
does not permit the evil of innocent suffering.

Might reluctance to grasp Plato's identification of the God with the
good come from attaching more importance to power than to love?
Casserley reverses these mistaken priorities:

For myself, I not only object to a conception of God that thinks of him
merely, or even primarily, in terms of sovereignty and power, but I
object also to any conception of man that thinks of him merely or even
primarily in terms of sovereignty and power, and I object to both
doctrines for the same reason, that they misapprehend the true value
and excellence of personality. The person, whether divine or human,
finds authentic self-expression in the range and integrity of his loving
and in the wide variety of his values.

(Casserley 1990: 27)

Chapter 11

Even if

Ethical truth can stand independently of religion. *Even if* God does not exist in reality and all religious symbols are brain products and nothing more, the fact that we are biologically capable of attaching ultimate importance to them attests to our essential value. *Even if* the Platonic good, the just, and the fair are illusions, a species capable of such illusions is worthy of respect. An idea's content, not its origin, bestows worth upon life if it is biologically constituted in such a way that it can apprehend symbols of such exceeding aesthetic magnitude.

Symbols of God, Platonic ideas, etc. *might* point to something that exists in reality, analogically reflect it, and allow us to participate in it. Roger Penrose's words are appropriate in this connection: "Plato himself would have insisted that the ideal concept of 'the good' or 'the beautiful' must . . . be attributed a reality . . . . Personally, I am not averse to such a possibility, but it has yet played no important part in my deliberations here" (Penrose 1994: 416).

The ideas might originate entirely within brains. Which ever of the two is the case *potentially* matters to religious faith, but not to foundational ethics. The aesthetic magnitude of the fugues of Johann Sebastian Bach, for instance, does not depend upon where it came from but upon the fact that it is. The brain/mind of a species structured by nature in such a way that it can bring rhythms and harmonies like these to consciousness makes the species valuable. *Even if* particular members of the species never hear such a fugue or, having heard it, repudiate it, this does not diminish their value. Ethics is essentially aesthetic if the core of aesthetics is the justification of existence. That core is music, but the musical rhythms and harmonies of consciousness include more than the fine arts. They subtend every life-affirming act that justifies existence aesthetically, including respect for scientific truth, tolerance, as well as love and beneficent thoughts, feelings, and actions. Once again, it is the neurobiological capability of these activities that bestows worth upon life.

Brain/mind contains the roots of respect for life, but the respect extends to body/mind as a whole, as I argue elsewhere: "The self is embodied and, as such, belongs to the body as a whole, not merely brain function" (Keyes 1991: 26). Furthermore,

> Brain function is the biological basis of personal individuality, namely our awareness of pleasure and pain, intellect, decision, and feelings previously attributed to the heart . . . . This attests both to the material nature of a person and to the symbolic meanings that make bodies different from all other kinds of matter.
>
> (Keyes 1991: 177)

This final argument of *Brain Mystery Light and Dark* attempts to recast the core of Immanuel Kant's *Foundations of the Metaphysics of Morals* into a naturalistic mode. To understand this it is first necessary to grasp his categorical imperative: "Act as though the maxim of your action were by your will to become a universal law of nature" (Kant 1969 [1785]: 39). In other words, we must extrapolate on what we intend to do and ask if we are willing for everyone to do it at all times and in all places. It is immoral to make an exception for ourselves that would go against our own universal legislation. Rational beings are capable of legislating in this way even though they do not always (and possibly rarely do) act accordingly. Kant's metaethical core follows from the need to respect beings that have this capability: "Act so that you treat humanity, whether in your own person or in that of another, always as an end and never as a means only" (Kant 1969 [1785]: 47). I change this to mean that life is essentially valuable because its neurobiological constitution makes conscience possible. He does not say this, but I argue that such an essentialist ethical interpretation can be defended, in spite of and to some extent on account of Paul D. MacLean's particular kind of professed relativism.

There are two types of ethical relativism. One is silly and the other true. I argue that MacLean's position is an instance of true relativism and also that it potentially passes over into essentialism, even though MacLean does not intend it to do so. Ethical relativism as such claims that all ethical judgments are reducible entirely to opinion, either private opinion (subjective relativism) or collective opinion (cultural relativism). Both private and cultural relativism can be either silly or true.

Silly relativism: self-certification

Relativism is silly when it ceases to be self-critical, fails to recognize that it is one theory alongside others, and becomes self-certifying. It traps itself in the Cretan paradox and cannot admit that it has done so. Ethical relativism says that there is only one ethical truth, namely that there is no ethical truth. This position is silly *unless* it openly acknowledges that its "one truth" contradicts itself. This failure in self-criticism might explain why relativists persistently mischaracterize essentialist theories. Entrapment in paradox, as opposed to acknowledgment of it, might be the blindfold that keeps it from seeing the processes from which ethical thinking originates.

Silly relativism can also slide into authoritarianism, despite its intent to do exactly the opposite. If the good is nothing but individual or social opinion, no standards of truth go beyond the individuals or social conventions that relativism says are the good's only sources. Nothing real can criticize the egotistical intolerance of the individual or the chauvinistic intolerance of the culture that decides what the good is. By reducing it to private opinion or social convention, relativism risks creating a vacuum that suffocates our ability to challenge potential demands that we conform. Relativism is neither silly nor vicious as long as it holds tolerance fast; but it seems to lose its ability to do this and starts turning into egotism and chauvinism the moment it ceases to be self-critical.

True relativism: completed self-reference

By contrast, true relativism is self-critical because it admits that it is entrapped in the Cretan paradox. MacLean, who inherits this paradoxical tradition through Bronowski, follows him in believing that the same endless regress that causes the problem of self-reference for mathematics and science also relativizes the truths of philosophy:

> It is clear enough that statements in philosophy are, by their nature, often dogged by self-reference, and that philosophy as a discipline is therefore limited even more severely than science by the logical gaps that the theorems of Gödel and Tarski have laid bare.
>
> (Bronowski 1966: 9)

In a statement published about a year later, MacLean states the ethical consequences of being caught in such an epistemological trap:

> Nothing is humanly more frustrating than to be caught in the trap of ignorance, and the prospect of never getting out of the trap makes some people dangerous to themselves. The ultimate inability to establish certitude of knowledge, however, need not apply to what we identify as 'values' which are, by nature, so relative and unmeasurable that they can never be known with certainty.
>
> (MacLean 1992: 57)

The problem of self-reference, MacLean's Second Trojan Horse, contains this paragon of true relativism, not only because it admits the contradiction, but also partly because he knows that the entrapment "makes some people dangerous to themselves." He says that not even limbic conviction can "nail down certitude" in the face of the "unyielding relativity" of values which the problem of self-reference generates. Doubt reaches a certain elegant perfection here.

I argue that this kind of doubt validates the doubter. Epimenides of Crete, out of whose tradition MacLean doubts, confesses that relativism contradicts itself when he says that all Cretans are liars. MacLean's concern about being trapped by unyielding relativity actually makes it yield. His concern is similar to the Cretan confession. It completes a circuit of self-reference. It inadvertently swims in the vortex where Douglas Hofstadter says all levels meet. Ultimate concern about entrapment liberates. It brings us to G.W.F. Hegel's true infinity out of the bad infinity of endless reflection in the hall of mirrors. The inviolate ethical order of true relativism is the value of the relativizer. Here, as elsewhere, the capability of valuation generates respect for life by looping back upon itself. This is the point at which relativism passes over into essentialism and vice versa.

The good, the just, and the fair

Plato's forms (ideas) are the ultimate paradigm of essentialism, whether aesthetic, religious, or ethical. His philosophy reverses ordinary priorities by attributing ultimate importance to the good, the just, and the fair. These are the inviolate Platonic order, neither private opinions nor social products.

As the Introduction to Part one explains, Plato's good is more than a model of behavior, even though it is also that. It is also more than the supreme object of mystical experience and happiness that overwhelms the liberated prisoner when he comes up from the underground dungeon from where he had been chained. The good is the source of knowledge and of being, and yet it "is still beyond being, exceeding it in dignity and power" (Plato 1968: 509B).

The fair and the just, essential aesthetic and ethical reality, come from the good. They are "really real" in comparison with physical things that participate in them and borrow their beauty and justice second hand:

> There exists an absolute beauty, and an absolute good, and an absolute greatness, and so on. If anything besides absolute beauty is beautiful, it is so simply because it partakes of absolute beauty . . . . I hold to the doctrine that the thing is only made beautiful by the presence or communication, or whatever you please to call it, of absolute beauty . . . it is absolute beauty which makes all beautiful things beautiful . . . no way in which a thing can be generated, except by participation in its own proper essence.
>
> (Plato 1951: 100B–01C)

Plato's theory of the forms survives the naturalistic recasting of his system after the destruction of body/soul dualism and its naturalistic recasting, as I have argued in Part one. It is logically consistent to argue that the brain/mind unity apprehends the forms symbolically. Such a position preserves the heart of the Platonic system while keeping the undivided unity of brain and soul. The real duality is between the brain/mind unity and the forms that go beyond it. The new, and distinctly different, question is: Do the good, the just, and the fair actually exist? Roger Penrose thinks that they might, even though he does not tie his physical hypothesis of consciousness upon that possibility. I stand where Penrose does, but also add something. *Even if* Plato's forms do not exist transcendently, having the illusion justifies the existence of the illusionist. Life capable of such illusions is worthy of respect.

Hypostatizing

Whether or not the Platonic forms exist, it might still be possible to identify the neurobiological processes that produce the conviction that they do. This would not tell us whether they are real or not, but it would reveal the processes of valuation that attest to the value of life. Steven Peterson hypothesizes how the brain might generate belief in the Platonic forms and other values to which it attributes external status.

Peterson suggests that we construct such ideas through a neurobiological process he calls "hypostatizing," which he defines as the normal human activity of treating values as if they were concrete, objective realities: "a process by which values, beliefs, and other human 'creations' become transmuted into 'things-in-themselves', and are considered apart from human activity" (Peterson 1983: 424). As a result, one thinks that the values are real "'outside oneself,' as independent entities, as Platonic forms," and this conviction tends to promote social stability, for "if there be mass consensus on a common set of hypostatized values within a society, stability is more likely to exist" (Peterson 1983: 424). He bases his explanation of hypostatizing upon MacLean's triune brain concept (prior to the decisive 1985 essay) as well as on a wide range of reports by other neuroscientists.

Rigidification

The basal ganglia, according to MacLean, are the source of such "reptilian" mental qualities as rigidity and the tendency to be "hidebound by precedent." He claims that the basal ganglia might contribute these qualities not only to instinctive tendencies, but to learned behavior as well. In the light of this, Peterson suggests that the basal ganglia could rigidify abstract notions: "People can come to cling jealously to tradition and habit and this might be generalized to ideals, beliefs, and values" (Peterson 1983: 430).

Organization

Functions such as collation of information and coordination of behavior might be based partly in the thalamus, according to Peterson. The thalamus, among other things, is a "way station" that relays impulses to the cerebral cortex from other brain centers, including the basal ganglia. Peterson cites various neuroscientists who suggest that the thalamus also has a role in correlating and integrating what it relays as well as focusing attention.

Furthermore, the thalamus might be a link between "rigidification" and "affect," partly because of its connection with the dorsomedial nucleus, which also projects to the basal ganglia. Peterson cites Talmage Peele, not MacLean, who writes that "the dorsomedial nucleus would appear to be involved in mechanisms underlying emotional expression" (Peele 1977: 293). Since the thalamus relays information collated "from a variety of areas" to the neocortex, Peterson claims that "The thalamus is likely to be a part of the system involved in organizing hypostatizing behavior" (Peterson 1983: 432).

Affect, interpretation, storage

The various structures of the limbic system contribute a variety of emotions, according to MacLean. The one affective quality to which Peterson calls attention is conviction. This is the feeling of urgent importance that MacLean says we attach to our beliefs, regardless of whether they are true or false. According to Peterson, it seems "to link the limbic system with affective coloration of hypostatized values or concepts" (Peterson 1983: 434).

The neocortex, organ of cognitive functions, is also "a partner in emotional processes," according to Peterson. He claims that the phylogenetically older structures mentioned earlier make important contributions to the higher cognitive functions. Peterson writes that "the limbic system produces primitive emotions and the neocortex interprets these" (Peterson 1983: 436). The hippocampus, a limbic structure, makes it possible for the neocortex to store long-term memories. Peterson thinks that the neocortex retains the hypostatizations together with the affective quality that the limbic system gives them. The neocortex can exercise some control over emotions. This is possible because of cortical-striatal, cortico-thalamic and cortico-limbic interconnections, according to Peterson. He writes that these pathways would allow for the conscious override or, if the social environment changes, the 'reprogramming' and 'reconditioning' of hypostatized values and beliefs and their effects . . . cortical efferents from integrative centers provide a theoretical basis for positing this override potential. Thus, there is a place for individual 'will' in this model.

(Peterson 1983: 440)

Internal reward system

Acting in accordance with hypostatizations that have been "rigidified and charged with affect" produces pleasure, Peterson writes. He cites James Danielli's hypothesis that there is an internal reward system that activates "euphorigenic" substances in the brain when human beings behave in a way consistent with their early conditioning. These substances are opiate peptides which have both an analgesic and a euphoric effect. They occur naturally in parts of the basal ganglia and limbic system, including the thalamus, and they appear to affect the way in which neurons fire in the hippocampus and neocortex. Peterson also cites Solomon Snyder: "The dorsal medial thalamus is strongly associated with frontal and limbic cortical areas involved in emotional regulation and so may relate to the euphoria produced by opiates" (Snyder 1978: 307; Peterson 1983: 438).

I argue that the origin of symbols is not what makes valuers valuable; they are worthy of respect because they are biologically capable of either apprehending or generating the ideas that the symbols express. To repeat, *even if* ideas like the good, the just, and the fair are brain products and nothing more, the existence of neurobiological structures within us that produce our concern about them makes us valuable. Since the human species is capable of having a conscience and being altruistic on account of the link between thalamocingulate structures and the pre-frontal lobes or for any other reason, then it is essentially worthy of respect. It follows from this that other species and life generally are worthy of various degrees of respect to the extent that it shares biological structures and functions which, in our species, bestow value upon life.[1]

Tolerance

Tolerance of difference also validates the valuer. I define tolerance as a type of behavior that bestows latitude and allows the other to be.

Hypostatizing can also lead to collective intolerance towards other societies. The "we–they"[2] distinction that this creates produces irrational nationalism, political conflict, and even warfare, according to Peterson. Hypostatizing can also lead to intolerance in smaller-scale interpersonal relations. Individual persons sometimes persecute others who do not share their hypostatized beliefs or whose behavior or type does not fit conventional models. In cases like these, intolerance seems to be a side-effect of hypostatizing. We could call this "chauvinistic intolerance." However, intolerance can also spring from the absence of hypostatizing. For instance, the egoist whose consciousness is de-hypostatized might be intolerant of others when they or their hypostatized values seem to thwart his will. We could call this "egotistical intolerance."

Just as intolerance has at least two sources, so does tolerance. First, tolerance is the opposite of chauvinistic intolerance because it permits the other to deviate from one's own (or group's) hypostatized values, life-styles, or stereotypes. It bestows latitude by "bracketing" the practical scope of those values without ceasing to believe them. Second, tolerance is the opposite of egotistical intolerance because it "brackets" the scope of one's own ego and makes room for others by renouncing the illusion of entitlement to use them. Both allow others to be through adjusting scope. They create latitude for others by arbitrating some kind of territorial metaphor belonging to what MacLean calls the R-complex. Tolerance overcomes the oppressive kind of reptilian rigidity on account of empathy for the other. It liberates another kind of reptilian rigidity, that of the well-mannered lizards.

To be tolerant is partly a rational decision to yield neither to destructive impulses towards others nor to excessive rigidity in making them conform to our own beliefs. Up to a point this seems to be neocortical override of certain reptilian drives and their limbic emotional elaborations. At the same time, the empathy that leads to tolerance seems to be more primitive than either hypostatization or override. Peterson suggests that suppressing dominance behavior, a requirement of tolerance, seem to involve all components of the triune brain, including the R-complex: "Centers that seem to suppress dominance behavior include the head of the caudate nucleus (part of the basal ganglia), a particular set of nuclei in the septum, and the *frontal lobes of the neocortex*" (Peterson 1988: 15–16).

Tolerance seems to be based largely on attitudes and types of behavior that fall outside the hypostatization process, but belief in tolerance could be hypostatized, for instance in the imperative to treat those whose ideologies differ from ours fairly. Such a concept is altruistic in its intent, tolerant in its effect, as well as beneficial both to the self and the other. We do not become unfaithful to our beliefs when we give others freedom not to be bound by them. Tolerance is letting the other be. It is therefore the covert truth of relativism. It is also the covert truth of essentialism in the sense that our capability of being tolerant makes us worthy of respect.

Epilogue: somehow to intervene

Our capability of alleviating suffering and preventing untimely death, not merely letting the other be, also makes us worthy of respect. Plato's *Republic* focuses on healing to illustrate just actions, since the physician's art aims at producing well-being and harmony within the recipient in an especially paradigmatic way. It is a model for beneficent action as such.

Attempting to heal also suggests that what *ought* to be sometimes corresponds with what *is*, and that to a certain extent we can derive the former from the latter. For instance, health ought to be and sometimes actually does exist. The way things actually are gives us significant, but limited, insight into what ought to be. Knowledge of the good, however, is only partly based on actuality. For the most part it is an aesthetic judgment that actual sickness of various kinds, both literal and metaphorical, ought not exist. Ethical action tries to turn what is into what ought to be.

Imperfection frustrates attempts to translate what ought to be into practical reality. As Hegel notes, to make any good concrete is to turn it into "a contingent, destructible existence, not a realization corresponding to its idea." The price we pay for externalizing the good is making it subject to "destruction by external contingency and evil" and to "collision and conflict" with some other good. In short, what ought to be has "inner infinitude," but it "cannot escape the destiny of finitude" (Hegel 1996 [1816]: 818–20).

Beneficent action requires courage in spite of the imperfection and even failure. Physicians, for instance, who heal now have failed before and are likely to do so in the future. Furthermore, healing is always temporary. Even when it succeeds, the same patient will probably suffer again and will certainly die. Also, during the stretch of time in which that particular patient's suffering is alleviated or death postponed, countless millions of others are undergoing unbearable suffering and meeting untimely death. Multiply all of this by time past and yet to come, and it will be clear that healing and all beneficent actions are statistically insignificant.

The courage of beneficence recognizes all of this, but reverses Hegel's dictum: *Even if* the good we intend "cannot escape the destiny of finitude," it nevertheless contains "inner infinitude" and that makes it ultimately important and eternally significant in spite of its quantitative unimportance. MacLean exposes that inviolate order:

> In the words of T.S. Eliot, we might imagine that 'The whole world is our hospital,' and we might continue with Howard Sackler's comment . . . that 'somehow to intervene, even briefly, between our fellow creatures and their suffering or death, is our most authentic answer to the question of our humanity.'
>
> (MacLean 1992: 70)

Make-a-man

Edited by Joseph Pawlosky

The strangest room in my childhood home in Ada, Oklahoma, was my father's study.

It was there, during the Second World War, that he taught me about the brain, and the most decisive lesson happened by accident while we played a game I had invented and named "make-a-man." That particular lesson was more or less a part of the private biology lectures he gave me every evening at dusk for several months before I started kindergarten.

A retired physician, he kept his surgical instruments, including a trephine used to bore holes in skulls, in an adjoining closet. He lined the walls with his medical library in long brown bookcases, each shelf covered by a folding glass door. Daddy organized every biology lesson around a picture in one of the volumes he kept there. Even though I hadn't yet learned to read, he taught me words like "eustacian tube" and "duodenum." Then I learned to identify words like these with the organ systems to which they belonged and to locate them in the pictures.

My father kept adding new books on neurology and neurosurgery to the brown bookcases during the eleven years between the beginning of my biology lessons and his death. The only way I can explain the meaning of what he taught me from those books is first to situate it in relation to some of the events that led up to its dawning. I still see him in that strange room, and my memory of him, still clear and sharply etched, brings flooding back my earliest awakenings to the brain and its workings. He is sitting there reading those books through a magnifying glass. A glaring light bulb attached to a grim looking out-of-date cord hangs all the way down to his chair.

Journeys

Robert Keyes had conceived me in his sixties when Ruth Brown, my mother, was in her late twenties. He was from Georgia, but *voluntarily* went out to Indian Territory, as Oklahoma was then known, to practice medicine. That was about 65 years after Andrew Jackson had forced the

Cherokees and other Indians to go there *involuntarily* on the death march called the Trail of Tears. He was the son of Delilah, a full-blood Cherokee. She was descended from a tribe whose members had managed to hold on to their eastern homelands in spite of everything. My father was practicing medicine near Okemah at the time Oklahoma became a state. Poor eyesight forced him into early retirement, first in Wewoka and then Ada, a few years before he married Ruth.

My own journeys are like braids that have connected much of the significance of my life, right from the start. Robert and Ruth conceived me in San Diego, California, and then drove 1,400 miles to Wewoka, Oklahoma, where I was born. Racial hybrids like me are at home there, my Native American constitution affecting not so much the way I look as the way I see.

Childhood memories of family automobile trips to the Gulf of Mexico, the Great Smokey, and the Rocky Mountains still live within me as conditioning influences on how I would view the world and my place in it. Summers in Colorado as a child and in New York as a teenager made me think of Ada as a homesite having a territorial range that extended from Pikes Peak on one end to Morningside Heights and the Cathedral of St John the Divine in Manhattan on the other. Looking back on those days, it was a challenge to maintain self-identity as that kind of cultural hybrid during the 1940s and 1950s.

My earliest memory fragment from that period goes back to 18 months of age. I distinctly recollect the cheerful sunshine and how happy my mother was as she nailed the numbers 1215 to the front of our new house in Wewoka. Her smile, the shape of those numbers, the hammer, and my joy have been a part of me ever since. So are many other scattered memories between then and age 5. My memories are largely intact from that time on. Possibly this is a blessing, though it might just as readily be a curse. Major events of the war came to be associated with certain stages of my education about the brain. At times I have wished I might be able to uproot everything I remember about the war, but tormented recollections of news reports and family attitudes towards it are still a part of me.

We moved 40 miles from Wewoka to Ada about a year after Pearl Harbor was bombed, not very long before playing make-a-man. Even though we had no relatives in the service and were not materially affected by the war, it was a constant emotional presence. As a boy of 6, I felt vulnerable despite the fact that we lived in the middle of the US. When Okinawa was invaded, I thought it was Konowa, a town 10 miles to the north. The European and Pacific fronts seemed to lurk all about the beautiful rolling hills that surrounded homesite Ada.

East Central State University, built on the edge of one of those hills, was only two blocks from our home, making the constant departure of young men and women to the war effort a common sight indeed. They called it

East Central State College in those days, and Horace Mann School, which I attended from kindergarten through high school, was a part of it. Some of my classes on the campus were held in Science Hall (Figure 6), an imposing building with stately white columns that seemed to invite confidence in reason. Two historically powerful objects guard access to that building from the main entrance to the campus. One is a memorial to students killed during the First World War. The other marker indicates

Figure 6 The Science Hall

that the fossilized remains of the Callixylon Tree next to it, dug up by a Choctaw Indian on his pig farm in 1930, was alive 250 million years ago. My appreciation of evolutionary time grew every time I read the marker. Over the years, it came progressively to situate me in my journey of discovery. The tree's remains were literally the center of my childhood education, located almost exactly midway between school and my home-based biology lessons, within sight of my father's study.

Threshold question

Make-a-man, the game we solemnly played in that strange room with the glaring light bulb, was spawned by my childish idea that anybody could make a complex object from ordinary parts. This illusion stayed with me for some time. Once I even tried to construct an airplane with boards for wings, coffee cans for engines, and rubbing alcohol for fuel. I planned it for several days ahead of time and believed in it enough that I was devastated when it didn't fly.

American forces were under attack and about to lose Corregidor the day I invented make-a-man. Spring had come to Ada. Its profuse beauty always made me restless. That particular afternoon, the outside of our stately brick home looked as bright as the inside of it looked strange. Snapdragons bloomed in the landscaped garden outside our home, and water lilies floated upon a pool made for them. Blackbirds pecked at the lawn late in the afternoon of the biology lesson that set the course of my life-long struggle to understand the brain. A strong wind drove them away and made the bus stop sign in front of the house creek with such a forlorn, eerie noise that I felt it urgent to go inside.

It was still light, but my father drew the curtains as if preparing for an air raid. Everything was dark in his study, except for the bare light bulb on its cord. I saw spots every time I looked away from it. That bulb was out of place in his study and didn't fit the house. Thinking of spring time outside made the light bulb and its dangerous looking socket seem even worse. It made my father's globe of the world reflect light in an odd way. The only other light in the study came from the dials on the short-wave radio. There was nothing on the radio except war news. My father leapt up and turned the radio off.

I jumped up and said, "Let's play make-a-man," and solemnly put flat boxes on the floor, one for each organ system from the lungs upward. The head was a shoe box. A leftover Christmas kit had several colors of sand in it, and I decided to put different colors in each box to stand for a different type of cell. I was so naive that I believed a person would spring forth if I used the right combination of sand. The game partook of magic and science at the same time. I made up the rules as we went along and explained the function of each organ system before I put the sand in the box that stood for it. Lungs and liver both got brown sand because I held back red for the heart. I paused in a ritual manner between explaining each organ and casting it in sand.

"The lungs draw oxygen in," I declared, and then asked, "How many cells are in the lungs?" My father told me he didn't know, "but put 30,000 to make a start." The heart pumps blood. "How many cells?" The liver purifies blood. "How many cells?" I sensed Daddy's patience was beginning to run out but couldn't understand why. He said, "40,000 to start making the heart and 50,000 for the liver." I couldn't believe how many cells it took even to start making a man and I knew I didn't have so much as a token amount of sand. Yellow was the only color left but I imagined the inside of the head was red. "How many cells for the brain?" I asked. My father answered, "10 billion for a start!" I threw all the yellow sand I had in the shoe box and asked, "Why do brains need so many cells? What does the brain do?" He looked straight at me and said, "The brain produces consciousness. It makes you see, hear, smell, taste, and feel. You think with your brain and your memories are stored in it." I looked down at the shoe-box head and a thin yellow strip of light seemed to come out. When I tried to stop it, the light hit the ceiling and slowly filled the room. I said to myself, "That's consciousness coming out of the brain."

It rained the next morning and Robert, my older brother, played the violin. I loved the rain because it always calmed my family down. The sound of rain going down the gutter and Robert's music made me happy. This mixture of sound also created a harmony that seemed to muzzle household anxiety for a little while. I went out onto the front porch to watch it rain and stroke my cat Rosie. In that brief space of time I formulated the question that never has left me: *How do brains produce consciousness*? What causes the leap from electro-chemical activity to my actual experience? What kind of mechanism pushes brain events over into my awareness of them? I now call this question the *threshold question*.

Vacuum in a bubble

The game that launched my life-long struggle to answer the threshold question also made me stop asking my father any more questions about brains. Strange feelings kept me from questioning what the brain does in the way that I questioned what the heart and liver did. I also sensed that some odd mixture of attraction and resistance was likewise coming from my father. When I got close to talking about brains, he reacted the same as when I tried to ask about sex organs. He had graduated from medical college in 1906. I now know that the scientific study of the brain was struggling to be born at that time and there was even disagreement whether there was synaptic transmission. That might explain why he hesitated to say much about the brain, even many years later. His silence about sex was probably a hold-over from the Victorian order. This combination of circumstances might explain why my pre-kindergarten biology lessons started with the digestive system, carefully worked up to the optic nerve, noting the brain's connection with it, and stopped there.

My knowledge of sexual physiology grew while my knowledge of the brain shrank. The threshold question remained unanswered, then as it does now. It bothered me more during grade school than it had before, since as my reading skill grew I became frustrated when I couldn't find answers in my father's medical library. So I secretly visited the physiology section of the university library to read about brains and sex organs. At home I drew diagrams of skeletons and all the organ systems from the digestive system to the eye. My clandestine trips to the library were a way of trying to extend my knowledge in two equally forbidden directions beyond the middle. The two were forbidden in different ways.

Sexual forbiddeness was mixed with sensual excitement and disorganized feelings of affection. At the same time, a sense of *familiarity* followed everything the physiology books taught me about sex and reassured me that it was in accord with nature. Brain function was the opposite, because a sense of *strangeness* always ran ahead of what I learned about it. This resistance constantly mixed itself with haunting fascination. Everything I read seemed unnatural. For instance, sensation and motor control of the left side of the body are based on the right side of the brain, and vice versa. Brain tissue itself has no sensation, but it causes sensation in the rest of the body. I asked myself, "If my brain makes me feel the pain in my finger, how does it make me feel the pain *there*?" Learning about brains seemed to be forbidden both before and after the fact. Every time I asked the threshold question, the space around the question got smaller and seemed to suffocate understanding. It felt like an airtight *vacuum in a bubble*.

Brain dread

A long time seemed to pass, long as childhood measures time, between the night of make-a-man and the day Daddy demolished my false belief that brains are invulnerable. I had acquired that illusion much earlier as an unintended consequence of a lesson Daddy taught me about the eye. He drew a diagram to illustrate how the lens turns the image upside down on the retina and explained that it and the optic nerve were connected to the brain. What I couldn't figure out was whether it was the retina or "something" inside the head that did the seeing.

My father then terrified me when he said that the eye is not solid at the center, but depends upon vitreous humor to hold it up. He told me the eye would go flat if it ever lost that liquid. I got sick when I learned that eyes are that fragile and not solid like marble, as I had believed. Brains, at least, were safely housed in bone. That thought made me feel better, and for years to come it put brains beyond the region of terror.

Some primitive dread came over me, however, even before I played make-a-man, when I thought of the inside of my own head. It is hard to explain exactly how I felt about the brain in those early days. The closest I can come is to say that I was naively thankful that the brain wasn't as fragile as the eye, since it was completely enclosed by the skull. My father told me that the optic nerves go into the brain through two openings in the bone. As a result, I pictured the brain as safely protected inside an oddly shaped fortress lying on the other side of the eyes with two small round windows and no door.

However, learning that all of the cells in the brain would die in a few minutes without oxygen put a real dent in my childish belief that the brain wasn't as fragile as the eyes. That illusion continued to crumble in the midst of my struggle with the threshold question, and my father destroyed it completely, without intending to do so, the day he showed me his surgical instruments and explained the purpose of all of them except, of course, those that had a sexual association. Frontier doctors practiced surgery as well as internal medicine, and he kept a variety of instruments in a shiny glass case in a small closet next to his library. I felt great curiosity and pride in how he had used those instruments to heal and to save lives. It was impossible for me to think that any of his patients ever died. I remember I wished he hadn't shown me the amputation saw, which caused me a peculiar apprehension. He explained each instrument I asked about until I pointed to an unusual pair of forceps which I later learned were used to deliver babies. But he clammed up and evaded every question that I asked about them. Finally I stopped and pointed to a drill and asked what it was for. He explained that it was a trephine and its purpose to make a hole in the skull for operations on the brain. Learning that the fortress surrounding the brain could be penetrated made me feel a genuine brain dread. A few months later my father told a story during dinner that added to my dread. I always enjoyed his stories and have continued to be fascinated by ones such as he told the night before about how some Indians in Georgia once hid from white soldiers by making themselves look like tree stumps and remaining motionless all night long. They sprang up at dawn and attacked the soldiers.

That night following, during dinner, he lectured on autopsies. It was totally consistent with his single-minded character to talk about such matters during meals, and nobody considered it improper. The pedagogical desert was an account of a particular autopsy he had performed after a shoot-out in front of a county courthouse soon after Oklahoma became a state. A man had died instantly after somebody shot him in the pelvis. Daddy explained that he had cut the corpse open and found that the bullet had hit a bone and been deflected into the abdomen. With total scientific detachment he explained how he had traced the bullet's path through the chest and into the neck. Then he cut the head in two and finally found the bullet in the middle of the brain. His point was only that bullets can be deflected by solid objects. As an afterthought he added that if I grew up to become a detective, as I hoped, I should carry two guns. The second gun was to be a small back-up weapon in case a criminal ever took my regular gun.

That night I slept more peacefully than usual, believing that I had just learned the secret of safety. Trading my primitive childish illusions about the fortress surrounding the brain for the newly acquired two-gun safety illusion made me feel secure for a short while; but two or three days later, I came to see what destruction of the earlier illusion meant. The dread this caused me was somewhat different from the terror I felt earlier about blindness and the fragility of the eyes. *Brain dread*, as I now call it, seemed more inexpressible. It felt like a burning coal buffered by some odd kind of icy denial. This new dread came to be the vacuum in the bubble.

Victory in Europe, Nazi revenge in Ada

Hitler committed suicide when I was 8 years old. The Allies' victory in Europe brought back some of my mother's happiness. Everyone in Ada rejoiced, or at least almost everyone did. Heidler,[1] a university student from out of state, was one of the exceptions. He was in some of Robert's classes and often came to the house. Heidler was a menace to my family. He irritated my mother by innuendo. One day she opened the door and he came in with her one piece of mail. "It's your church bulletin," he said. "I'm sure you're eager to read it." He used to brag that his name sounded like "Hitler." My father said he might be a Nazi spy.

For some reason, Heidler seemed to hate me more than he did the rest of my family. He was always snooping around the house. About a year before Hitler's defeat, he somehow found out that I was afraid of blindness. One evening he called me on the telephone and told me to listen to Gangbusters on the radio because it was going to be an "interesting radio program tonight." It turned out to be about a criminal who blinded somebody. He gouged the victim's eyes out with a paper knife. The next day Heidler came by and asked how I liked the program. He didn't wait for an answer but smiled and gleefully described details of the Nazi bombing of London. Keyes was obviously an English name, and somebody must have told him I had Cherokee blood as well. That might have made him hate me more, but I wasn't a very convincing Indian with blonde hair. He liked calling me "*Red*-headed Schweinkopf," but always buffered that nickname in a joke and said I wasn't supposed to take it seriously.

Not long after the war ended in Europe, my parents drove to Oklahoma City one afternoon. Robert and I stayed in Ada. It was raining when I came home from school, and I hoped he would be playing the violin, but he didn't answer when I called upstairs. My cat Rosie seemed upset. I heard noises coming from Robert's room and thought he must be playing hide-and-seek. The fact that the curtains were closed confirmed my suspicion. So I jumped in and said, "Caught you!" The door slammed behind me and Heidler's voice said, "To be strictly correct, I've caught a Redhead. I'm going to show you something." He pulled a chair in front of the door to trap me inside and turned the light on.

Heidler was wearing a complete Nazi S.S. uniform. He saluted, barked, "Heil Hitler," and sat down. "I'm going to teach you some things. See this ring? The white part is made of the teeth of Russians. The silver we pulled out of the fillings of Frenchmen." He must have known about the trace of French blood on my mother's side. Heidler switched on a strange lamp I had never seen before. "Look at this lamp. It's made of the skin of Jews. And I've got something for your head." He poked at a bulge in his left coat pocket and slowly pulled out a shiny object with his right hand. It was my father's trephine! Heidler said, "I'm going to bore a hole in your *red* head." That terrified me into paralysis. He came at me twisting the trephine. "I'll put the hole in the upper left side of your skull, so you won't be able to talk about it." When he got within an inch of me, he slowly backed off and didn't say anything else. He put on a rain coat, hid his cap and that ghastly lamp under it, and walked out into the rain without ever touching me.

Rosie wildly scratched a chair in the next room until a loud clap of thunder drove her under it. The trephine was on the floor between Rosie's hiding place and my old phonograph, a hand-operated device with the only record my parents gave me, Beethoven's "Minuet in G." I took the trephine and bored a hole in the wall with it. Then I put it back in my father's surgical cabinet and straightened up Robert's room. Everything looked normal except for the hole in the wall next to the *Encyclopaedia Britannica*. Robert finally came home, and he asked me what was wrong. I told him I was worried about him, which was true. He said that Heidler had switched plans at the last minute about where to review for finals and then didn't show up. Later my family was relieved to hear that Heidler had disappeared. In a few days my mother found the hole. She was extremely disturbed and asked me if I had shot a hole in the wall. "No," I said, "I bored a hole in it." I still cannot understand why she didn't scold me but simply dropped the subject with that explanation without even asking why and how I had done it. If only she had pressed me, I might have told her the whole story and relieved my mind. As a result, I never told anyone what happened that bizarre afternoon, but her question did implant a deep desire in me to shoot a hole in that wall.

Visit to Oklahoma City

On 6 August 1945, my parents and I went to Oklahoma City. I always liked going there. The tall buildings and street cars, which Ada didn't have, excited me. Oklahoma City was also culturally different in a subtle way. Ada had belonged to Indian Territory and felt like a western outpost of the old south. By contrast, the City, as we called it, built on the flat land of Oklahoma Territory at what seemed truly the threshold of the wild west, had more of the look of the Midwest about it. It had a kind of urbanity all its own. Those characteristics, the interurban line to the University of Oklahoma in Norman, and a flourishing petroleum economy made travel to Oklahoma City seem like a more radical journey than it actually was.

That particular day we were walking south on Hudson Street when my father told me that the center of Hiroshima had been destroyed by an atomic bomb, a new kind of weapon that vaporized its target. At that moment, it registered with me not as a military victory but as a new type of terror. I looked down an alley to my right and saw the old county courthouse, an ornate, older building some distance off, and I remember dreading that it, too, could be vaporized. For a moment I visualized an atomic bomb exploding over Oklahoma City. Ada might be safe, but certainly not the City! That dreadful vision of the vaporizing of the courthouse and the lesson in finitude it taught never left me, not even years later after I learned that it had been dismantled in 1950.

The feeling of dread that was spawned by such a vision was not entirely to be quieted with that dismantling. Like a specter ever intent on making its presence known, the same feeling would rise up and catch me unawares on 19 April 1995. I was about to begin a lecture on the problem of innocent suffering when one of my students angrily entered the classroom and announced that the federal building in Oklahoma City had just been bombed. Reports that followed from the "threshold of the wild west" brought vividly back the memory of the visit that day with my parents and of my father's reporting the atomic bomb's vaporization of Hiroshima. Some might suggest that in picturing the vaporization of the courthouse that day, years before the federal building was even to be built, I may have had some kind of premonition, but I rather think it more likely to have been a tragic coincidence.

During the drive back to Ada following the visit with my parents, I felt a mixture of joy that the war was ending, along with an unbounded curiosity about how the bomb worked. I read everything I could find on physics and talked to my teachers in school and to university professors who came to dinner until I finally grasped the mechanism of nuclear fission and spontaneous chain reactions. Nobody told me about civilian casualities in Hiroshima and Nagasaki until much later, and then denial took control again when I started picking up fragments of information about the atrocity. I grasped it by degrees along with the nuclear threat to the continued existence of the human race. These concerns didn't stop my interest in science and my naive belief that technology could solve most human problems.

The fact that I gained a childish understanding of the mechanism by which the bomb worked made me think that everything must be caused by some kind of mechanism. That once again stirred within me the *threshold question* and confirmed my belief that there had to be a brain mechanism that produces my awareness of what I experience.

Oscillation hypothesis

During junior high school, I wondered whether the brain processes in question operated like an electronic circuit. I gave up drawing skeletons and started drawing, and then trying to build, simple electrical and electronic circuits. At first I drew diagrams of telephone circuits and made primitive telephones. Then I did the same with amplifiers, receivers, transmitters, and *oscillators*. I understood the basic mechanisms by which oscillators produce sound. Is there some kind of high level oscillator inside my head, I wondered, that did a similar thing? Did brain events cross the threshold into my awareness of them by feeding back into themselves?

War surplus radio parts flooded Ada then, and this led to an odd chain of events that pushed my fantasies about electromagnetism and the brain off the deep end. The white limestone armory was filled with an unimaginable variety of components and exciting switch-covered black boxes from planes and ships. I bought as many parts as I could afford, including a prize 2,000-volt transformer. It was the center of everything I did for about a week, but nobody knew I had it. It was interesting because it was dangerous. Since I didn't have any existing use for that exotic transformer, I invented one. I was limited by the small inventory of parts that I had and the few I borrowed from Robert. As a result, I designed and built a receiver circuit around voltage at the expense of purpose. I didn't even know its frequency range. When nobody was at home, I disconnected the antenna to the family short wave radio and hooked it up to my machine. The lights flickered when I turned it on. At first there was an appalling silence, not even the hum I expected, but the moment of truth came at the lower end of the dial. I overheard both sides of a telephone conversation. Of course, it could have been a car telephone, even though they were rare in those days. I wondered whether telephone lines might give off electromagnetic signals that could be monitored.

Then my pre-adolescent imagination leapt to another level and ran wild with a new question. Might brains also transmit electromagnetic fields? If they did, couldn't the right kind of receiver then pick them up? I built an elaborate technological fantasy world around those thoughts. Brain monitoring would be used for one purpose only, to prevent war. The tragedy of deploying the atomic bomb by America was starting to catch up with me. For the most part, I turned these my fantasies about brain electromagnetism inward and talked about them only once when I was a child. I regretted telling an insensitive boy in school about my proposed "brain machine." He said, "It won't work; brains are only red meat inside heads."

Winter of despair

My grandmother had a stroke that winter. Mama, as my mother and the rest of my family called her, lived with us. I had read a lot about strokes and knew what they were in the abstract. Mama told me what it felt like. She got a headache and felt dizzy in the kitchen and walked upstairs to lie down. The trip up to her bed seemed to take several hours. She said time stood still for quite awhile and when she lay down her left side turned numb and was paralyzed. I immediately figured out which part of the right side of her brain had been destroyed, but a vacuum of icy disbelief settled like a bubble around what I had figured out and what Mama told me. I was thankful the stroke hadn't affected her mind. She even helped me with my homework.

One night during a study break, I read a popular article about Harvey Cussing, a pioneer brain surgeon. It mentioned some of the techniques he had used to save lives. Despite the life-affirming tone of the article, it, along with what Mama told me, seemed to enter into a strange emotional conspiracy against my peace of mind. Together they finished the dismantling of my childish illusion that brains were not as vulnerable as eyes. Not only can the fortress that surrounds the brain be penetrated or opened, but accidents can happen even inside a skull that is safe externally. My father's scientific lessons and Heidler's sadistic lesson sank in. As a result, this new emotional conspiracy turned brain dread into persistent, obsessive thoughts. Mama died less than a year later.

Ura became my surrogate grandmother. After all, she was my oldest living friend. She seemed eternally old, unchanged by time both before Mama died and decades later. This dignified lady from Mississippi had lived in Wewoka, knew my parents there before I was born, and moved to Ada ahead of us. Ura embodied wisdom, for she neither prejudged a matter nor spoke platitudes. Ura also faithfully read the Bible. All of this drove me to ask her, "Does God make evil things happen?" She instantly replied, "No." Then I asked, "Does God *let* them happen? Did he *let* Mama have a stroke? Did he *let* Truman bomb Japan?" Ura hesitated a long time before she said, "There isn't any answer to those questions."

Aesthetic conversion

An interlude of peace followed grief, and I had the illusion that it would last forever. I enjoyed life during the twilight of my pre-adolescence by riding my bicycle and swimming. The town I loved was suddenly mine because I could ride anywhere except downtown. It was fun to coast down steep residential streets and see tree-covered hills in the distance beyond palatial white limestone houses. The Ada rodeo was well-known in the west, and the cowboys who crowded into town were connected to their horses differently than I was to my bicycle. Their way of riding seemed superior to mine.

My swimming coach was from the university athletic department. He taught boys my age swimming lessons in the campus pool and impressed us by swallowing whole cigarette butts. The university music school had a horn practice room next to the pool in the gymnasium, and that extended my grasp of music, which grew beyond Beethoven's "Minuet in G." Mozart's horn compositions accompanied almost every swimming class. His music became so much my own that I felt I could taste it. That might have been a subjective reaction against the thought of eating tobacco, but whatever it was prepared me for the most decisive music lesson of my life.

The university chorus happened to practice with windows open in Science Hall the same day I was studying a book on electronic systems in the building next to it. A gentle autumn breeze blew through the open window and ruffled the curtain. All at once there was music absolutely new to me. It welded rationality and intense passion, feelings I later identified as the beautiful and the sublime, into one inseparable whole. This had nothing to do with the exceptional expertise of the singers; they were obviously skipping around and working on particular parts of something. My experience also had nothing to do with the words they sang, either, since I didn't recognize them and barely even heard them. Whatever the words were, they merely rode the rhythm and harmony, neither the way I did my bicycle nor the way a cowboy rides a horse, but more the way a flea would.

My musical experience that sunshiny afternoon consisted less in what I heard than in what I *saw*. I didn't see the undivided unity of intellect and emotion in the same way that I saw the curtain; nor was there any semblance of actual or hallucinated perception. I didn't fantasize anything that I might have perceived or imagined before. Something that goes beyond all those ways of seeing crashed through the window. Pure rhythm flung chord structures more massive than boulders into space, caught them, and held them in an ordered grasp. Many tunes light-heartedly played with one another and frolicked in a solemn unity from which none could have been removed without destroying the whole.

This is a blood and guts aesthetics. Even though it includes the sublime, it is not "mystical." It frolicked too much to call it that. Something extraordinary happened to me, but it neither took me out of ordinary life nor distracted me from it. On the contrary, the primal aesthetic experience justified it. Later I found out that the chorus was practicing a cantata of Johann Sebastian Bach's.

Season of compulsion

I often rode my bicycle home from the gymnasium as fast as I could to listen to Indian dances on WNAD from the University of Oklahoma. Mother looked devastated one day when I came home from the gymnasium, and that ended the interlude of peace. She said that Daddy had suffered a stroke and was in the hospital. It took a while for thought and feeling to catch up with what she had said. While I struggled to focus, I asked her almost mechanically which side of his body was paralyzed. She said he wasn't paralyzed anywhere, but that the "stroke destroyed his mind." I wasn't allowed to visit him in the hospital because he wouldn't recognize me. The next week they brought him home. He looked normal in every way and could walk, eat, and talk, but when he did talk, he spoke nonsense. In his youth he helped found a state. When he retired he taught me biology. Now he only muttered incoherent, obscene half-sentences. Daddy never acknowledged me personally until the last few seconds before he died in the hospital 18 months later. He regained consciousness in what seemed to be the only lucid moment that he had since the stroke. Then, in the instant before he died, he looked straight at me and said, "My son."

A powerful emotional force drove me to read about brain surgery in my father's medical library during his illness and for some time after he died. It might be easy for common sense to see how his devastating stroke caused me to have this compulsion. As for myself, I did not, and still do not, feel any connection. An observer is always free to see causes from the outside, but they are often opaque to the person required to live their effects from the inside.

My compulsion started one afternoon when I looked at the hole I had bored in the wall and thought of Heidler. I remembered that my mother asked me if I had shot the hole and that renewed my desire to shoot a hole in something. Then I started wondering what would have happened if I had shot Heidler in the head instead of boring a hole in the wall. Maybe it wouldn't have killed him, because I remembered that there are some "silent areas" of the brain, but where were they?

The *Encyclopaedia Britannica* stood next to the telling hole I had bored. I looked up the article on the brain in an effort to figure out which area did what. A following article was on surgery of the brain, and it caught my attention because I wondered what it would take to remove a bullet from Heidler's brain. Two hours later I started systematically going through my father's library. Some of the same books that had delighted me nine years before when he taught me biology now turned against me. Unquenchable need consumed me when I did not read them. These two slave masters of dread and need ruled my waking life. Sleep became my only freedom. I remember being surprised that I slept so soundly and never dreamed about what I did by day. Each morning I woke up with renewed energy, which dread and need then would devour.

The good, the just, and the fair

Time lost its meaning in those days because my struggle seemed endless. In reality, though, the epoch of despair I have just described both began and ended during the midnight of my pre-adolescence. A short stretch of nature can house a bad eternity when unquenchable dread and need consume a life, yet it was nature that liberated me. Puberty came over night. No dawn preceded it. Many years before, I saw university students making out all over the campus, and I asked my parents why. They laughed and said, "Just wait. You will understand." I believed them because they sounded so convincing, but I supposed the change would be gradual. That belief and my boundless curiosity about sex were not connected to one another, not even on the last night before puberty. When I went to sleep, there was no hint that an abrupt hormonal change would kill my peculiar obsession before morning. I went from the midnight of dread to the bright dawn of sexual desire in less than eight hours. The need for a girlfriend put the urgency of my question about the brain to sleep for a while.

A strange turn of events introduced me to metaphysics about the same time. I went to the university book store to buy a baseball bat, because they had the best selection in Ada. Then, on the way home, I stopped at Tuck's Drug Store to look at the paperback books, hoping to find something about sex. Instead I bought Jowett's translation of the *Dialogues* of Plato, and went home with it in one hand and the bat in the other. Plato's account of Socrates' trial, imprisonment, and execution inflamed my interest in everything I loved. His account of the good, the just, and the fair in the *Republic* made life on this earth seem more valuable than it had before. It cast a new kind of light that changed the way the world looked. I felt less hemmed in. Social injustice suddenly looked more evil and the need to change the world more urgent. Plato's good turned me into a frustrated lone wolf civil rights activist in high school. Almost nobody listened to anything I had to say about racial equality. That isolated me from the community and also increased my concern about ethical issues. The cold war, the possible annihilation of the human race, and the problem of suffering begged for answers. That was when I decided to study philosophy with Gustav Mueller, and the classics at the University of Oklahoma.

The belly dancer and the grave yard

My frustration with sex increased as my world grew in size. After my father died, my mother and I went to New York by train every summer. She was as awkward talking about sex as he had been and evaded the subject every time I brought it up. There was a story in *Life* one summer about an exotic Turkish belly dancer about to make her American debut at a Manhattan night club. I clipped the photographs and looked at them constantly. Without explaining why, I somehow managed to talk my mother into making reservations at that very night club before we left New York. She was as obviously shocked with the performance as I was pleased. Afterwards, she said she couldn't believe how "forthright" the dancer had been. I told her I was not surprised and confessed that I had asked her to make the reservations because I already knew about the dancer. Mother looked exasperated and amused at the same time, and I felt there would be a reaction, but I had no idea it would plunge me even further into metaphysics.

Later that summer, when we visited San Diego briefly, Mother took me to Amnherst Street and showed me a house with a tile roof surrounded by palm trees. She told me that was where she and Daddy lived before they moved to Wewoka. Then she pointed to a shutter-covered window and said, "You were conceived in that room. I'll tell you the rest of the story when we get back to Ada." I was curious about what she was going to say, but I had learned not to raise certain questions. A few days after we returned to Ada, she asked me to drive her to the cemetery. An explorer who had passed through that area in 1884 described the hills on the horizon: "Yesterday we traveled mostly across forest and rocky broken country, today we go over some charming dales, we climb some sunny flowery hillsides" (McKeown 1980: 5). We saw Mama's grave first and then my father's. Mother pointed to a plot close to his and gently said, "You were conceived in San Diego. And this will be your grave after you die." I looked out towards the rolling hills and asked myself if there was anything beyond death.

Callixylon tree revisited

Though having had several personal encounters with death in the 1960s, it was not until some years later that I would come to be taught, without their intending it, what my own death means by my undergraduate students at Duquesne University. Some of those earlier encounters included looking down the barrel of somebody's else's loaded gun, two close calls in private planes, a boating accident, and a devastating car wreck in 1965 that resulted in my right carotid artery being pierced. I felt depressed about being through the windshield as a passenger, while the earlier near catastrophes merely evoked excitement.

None of those incidents allowed me "to see" death as truly *my own*, any more than did my extreme grief over my mother's death in 1981. But Duquesne students in my Philosophy of Sex class, my favorite course, destroyed the illusion that had blocked me from situating myself in the rhythm of time that leads forward to my appointed grave in Ada. My illusion was a ghost of the childish belief that children are always young, the elderly always old, and that the stages between are similarly fixed. It followed, then, that college students were changelessly fixed as youthful adults. My experience supported this view, because that is how the students seemed throughout the 12 years or so that I had watched them making out on all sides of the Callixylon tree. Then I graduated from high school and became one of them myself at the University of Oklahoma.

Then, years later, when I started teaching courses on the Philosophy of Sex, I discovered that undergraduates were *still* youthful adults. Hundreds of such changelessly fixed students took this course as the decades came and went. No matter how many times a week I might forget where I had parked my car, other memories, such as where specific students had sat in class and exactly how they looked as young adults, would be indelible. Then all of a sudden I started running into some of those on the streets in Pittsburgh at fast food stores and on the Pennsylvania Turnpike. Some were middle aged! Time had changed *them*, but, of course, not me.

As it happened, I went one year to Ada to visit Ura. She was my oldest friend and had always seemed elderly. The fact that Ura looked relatively unchanged after so many years was momentarily reassuring, until she said to me in an affectionate way, "Don, you have aged beyond belief!" That was the last time I saw Ura, because she died soon afterward. But I visited the Callixylon tree before I left Ada, when Ura and I finished talking. After all, it was the center of my earlier education.

The tree that marks a point in biological time that runs forward also provokes us to remember what came before. The same narrative has a past that stretches back from us through 4 billion years to life's beginning on earth. Even though that is an abysmal length of time measured by frailty, it is short in comparison with the 18 billion year stretch back to the Big Bang. Furthermore, the universe is 18 billion light years wide and still expanding. Our vulnerability has a cosmic dimension that is both anxiety provoking and reassuring. Step back and watch our mortal planet orbit an insignificant star in an obscure part of the cosmos long enough and it will put your own death in place. Our fragile brains are precariously staged on a fragile earth for a fleeting instant, and the story of that brain is the story of us, the story of who and what we are as a species and as individuals, the story of our dawning awareness of our emergence into time and our passing out of it. It is, in a word, the story of all stories.

Notes

Chapter I The fortress

1 This section is based, in part, on my essay "Crisis of brain and self" (Keyes 1996).

2 Colin McGinn argues that the problem of the relation between brain and mind is therefore a philosophical illusion in Wittgenstein's sense (McGinn 1991: 84). McGinn writes that consciousness has a "natural depth" and a "concealed underside" like a "pyramid only the tip of which is visible – a pyramid equipped with elaborate internal workings, scarcely imaginable from what is given" (McGinn 1991: 91). The hidden natural depth of conscious states

> mediates between their surface properties and the physical facts on which they continually depend. The surface properties are not enough on their own to link consciousness states intelligibly to the physical world, so we need to postulate some deep properties to supply the necessary linkage. Some properties *must* exist to link consciousness intelligibly to the brain, since it is so linked; my suggestion is that these properties belong to the hidden nature of consciousness.
>
> (McGinn 1991: 100)

Thomas Nagel catalyzes McGinn's thinking in what seem to be two distinctly different ways. On the one hand, McGinn's position seems to be directed towards Nagel's concern about the "irreducible subjectivity of the mental." Nagel writes:

> For if the facts of experience – facts about what it is like *for* the experiencing organism – are accessible only from one point of view, then it is a mystery how the true character of experiences could be revealed in the physical operation of that organism.
>
> (Nagel 1974: 442)

On the other hand, Nagel's "dual aspect" theory of the relation between mind and brain (Nagel 1986: 28–32) seems to be the thesis of McGinn's antithesis that the structure of consciousness is hidden. Nagel holds that there are two levels, one physical and the other phenomenological. McGinn interprets Nagel to mean that subjective states are themselves physical conditions and that consciousness consists in brain states. He believes Nagel's position would leave open "a blank space which may be subsequently filled by science; mental concepts likewise contain a blank that neurophysiology will eventually fill" (McGinn 1991: 102). McGinn's rejection of this position clarifies more than one would expect:

> The kind of hidden structure I envisage would lie at neither of the levels suggested by Nagel: it would be situated somewhere between them. Neither phenomenological nor physical, this mediating level would not (by definition) be fashioned on the model of either side of the divide, and hence would not find itself unable to reach out to the other side.
>
> (McGinn 1991: 103–4)

I argue on the contrary not only that we cannot split the "two levels" of the dual aspect theory but that we need to pull them even closer together into a more solid identity.

3 This position does not rule out the possibility of viewing life after death as replication. I am planning a new book that will address this question in the light of the conclusions of the present one.

Chapter 2 Light and dark

1 Chapter 2 is based, in part, on my essay "Paul D. MacLean's triune brain hypothesis: which platonic metaphor fits and which does not?" (Keyes 1997).

Part two: Beasts within

1 Chapters 3 and 4 are based, in part, on my essay "Ethical judgment and brain function: an interpretation of Paul D. MacLean's hypothesis" (Keyes 1992).

Chapter 4 Conviction and conscience

1 J. Bronowski writes, commenting on the problem of self-reference in Kurt Gödel's theorem:

> In 1931 a young Austrian mathematician, Kurt Gödel, proved two remarkable and remarkably unwelcome theorems. The first theorem says that any logical system which is not excessively simple (that is, which at least includes ordinary arithmetic) can express true assertions which nevertheless cannot be deduced from its axioms. And the second theorem says that the axioms in such a system, with or without additional truths, cannot be shown in advance to be free from hidden contradictions. In short, a logical system which has any richness can never be complete, yet cannot be guaranteed to be consistent . . . . I hold, therefore, that the logical theorems reach decisively into the systemization of empirical science . . . . The laws of nature cannot be formulated as an axiomatic, deductive, formal and unambiguous system which is also complete.
>
> (Bronowski 1966: 3–5)

Bronowski acknowledges that the "endless regress" of his "hall of mirrors" goes back to Epimenides:

> And the regress comes sharply to a focus in all the paradoxes of logic, which are cousins of one sort or another to the classical contradiction that

the Greeks knew: what they called the Cretan paradox. This is the contradiction implied by the statement of Epimenides the Cretan that all Cretans are liars .... The mathematical paradoxes, and the devices derived from them that Gödel and others exploited for their theorems, all have the same feature: they depend on the use of concepts whose range of reference includes the concept itself. In short, the model for them all is the Cretan paradox, the simple sentence, 'What I am now saying is not true.' This is obviously a self-contradiction: if the assertion is true, then by its own evidence it is not true; and if the assertion is false, then that tells us that what is being said must be true.

(Bronowski 1966: 7–8)

2 According to Paul D. MacLean, space and time are no yardstick by which the problem of self-reference can be overcome, for they "do not exist *per se* but are purely informational constructs derived by the subjective brain." In other words, as Kant has shown, space and time are *a priori* intuitions. MacLean writes:

Space in his scheme belongs to the 'outer sense' and time to the 'inner sense'. Similarly, he ascribed to the 'understanding' the *a priori* functions that give form to what is intellectually experienced. Thus, he contended that both the 'form of sensibility' (otherwise referred to as the *transcendental aesthetic*) and 'pure understanding' are necessary for the appreciation of total experience. One might say that like a television tube without a screen, there could be no picture of experience without these *a priori* formal properties of the mind and senses. Hence, it can be argued that time and space do not exist *per se* but are purely informational constructs derived by the subjective brain.

(MacLean 1990: 570–1)

Chapter 9 Near life experiences

1 This chapter is based, in part, on my book *God or Ichabod? A Non-Violent Christian Nihilism* (Keyes 1973) and my essay "Crisis of brain and self" (Keyes 1996).

Chapter 10 God and evil

1 This chapter is based, in part, on my book *God or Ichabod? A Non-Violent Christian Nihilism* (Keyes 1973), my essay "Crisis of brain and self" (Keyes 1996), and my internet essay "Christian faith for the 21st century," web site of the Church of the Transfiguration, New York: **http://littlechurch.org** (Keyes 1997).
2 The use of this term to refer to religious faith was suggested by Hans Urs von Balthasar (1983 [1969]: 135–53).

Chapter 11 Even if

1 The "perceptive critic" asks: "If beings are not yet biologically capable of either apprehending or generating the ideas the symbols express could they not still be 'essentially valuable'? How is 'essential value' determined and defined? As an example, don't species other than our own have 'essential value'?" (Demas 1997: 1).
2 The same critic also asks: "As an instance of the problem of the we–they

distinction, could the hypostatizing that causes intolerance of other societies also cause collective intolerance of other species? The we/they distinction risks becoming irrational human chauvinism that can only interpret other life forms in terms of utility. We/they then becomes we/it" (Demas 1997: 1).

Epilogue

1 The name "Heidler" is purely fictitious and bears no resemblance to the actual name of the person in question. Any similarity this name might have to any person living or dead is purely coincidental. The events pertaining to him are factual in every detail, except that they compress two or three actual episodes into one.

Bibliography

Aristotle (1965) *Poetics*, trans. W. Fyfe, in *Aristotle, The Poetics, "Longinus" On the Sublime, Demetrius On Style*, Cambridge, MA: Harvard University Press.

Ashbrook, James (1989) "The whole brain as the basis for the analogical expression of God," *Zygon: Journal of Religion and Science* 24 (March): 65–79.

Baars, Bernard (1997) *In the Theater of Consciousness, The Workspace of the Mind*, New York: Oxford University Press.

Baars, Bernard and McGovern, Katharine (1996) "An introduction to the science of consciousness," in Max Velmans (ed.) *The Science of Consciousness: Psychological, Neuropsychological and Clinical Reviews*, New York: Routledge, pp. 63–95.

Back, George (1995) "Emergency letter to parish in response to the Murrah Building Bombing," No. 1, unpublished.

Balthasar, Hans von (1983 [1969]) *Convergences to the Source of the Christian Mystery*, trans. E.A. Nelson, San Francisco, CA: Ignatius Press.

Berdyaev, Nicolas (1960 [1931]) *The Destiny of Man*, trans. Natalie Duddington, New York: Harper and Row.

Bible, The Holy, Westminster Study Edition (1958) Philadelphia: Westminster Press.

Bloom, Alan (1988) *The Closing of the American Mind*, New York: Simon and Schuster.

Boitano, John (1996) "Edelman's biological theory of consciousness," in S. Hameroff, A. Kaszniak, and A. Scott (eds) *Toward a Science of Consciousness*, Cambridge, MA: MIT Press, pp. 113–19.

Borchgrevenk, Hans (1982) "Prosody and musical rhythm are controlled by the speech hemisphere," in Manfred Clynes and Janice Walker (eds) *Music, Mind, and Brain: the Neuropsychology of Music*, New York: Plenum Press, pp. 151–8.

Bronowski, J. (1966) "The logic of the mind," *American Scientist*, Spring-March: 1–15.

Calvin, William (1983) *The Throwing Madonna*, New York: McGraw Hill.

—— (1990) *The Cerebral Symphony*. New York: Bantam.

Camus, Albert (1955 [1942]) *The Myth of Sisyphus and Other Essays*, trans. Justin O'Brien, New York: Vintage.

Casserley, Julian (1960) *Christian Community*, New York: Longmans, Green.

—— (1990) *Evil and Evolutionary Eschatology: Two Essays*, C. Don Keyes (ed.), Lewiston, NY: Edwin Mellen Press.

Churchland, Patricia (1986) *Neurophilosophy: Toward a Unified Science of the Mind-Brain*, Cambridge, MA: MIT Press.

Clynes, Manfred and Walker, Janice (eds) (1982) *Music, Mind, and Brain: The Neuropsychology of Music*, New York: Plenum Press.

Cooney, Brian (1991) *A Hylomorphic Theory of Mind*, New York: Peter Lang Publishing Inc.

Crick, Francis (1995) *The Astonishing Hypothesis: The Scientific Search for the Soul*, New York: Simon and Schuster.

Danielli, James (1980) "Altruism and the internal reward system or the opium of the people," *Journal of Social Biological Structures* 3: 87–94.

d'Aquili, Eugene (1983) "The myth–ritual complex: a biogenetic structural analysis," *Zygon: Journal of Religion and Science* 18 (September): 247–69.

—— (1986) "Myth, ritual and the archetypal hypothesis," *Zygon: Journal of Religion and Science* 21 (June): 141–60.

Demas, Rebecca (1996) written correspondence, unpublished.

—— (1997) written correspondence, unpublished.

Deminkov, V. (1962) *Experiments in the Transplantation of Vital Organs*, New York: Consultants Bureau.

Demos, Raphael (1937) intro. to *The Dialogues of Plato*, Vol. 1, trans. B. Jowett, New York: Random House.

Dennett, Daniel (1991) *Consciousness Explained*, Boston: Little, Brown.

Durant, John (1981) "The beast in man: a historical perspective on the biology of human agression," in Paul Brain and David Benton (eds) *The Biology of Aggression*, NATO Advanced Study Institute Series, Rockville, MD: Sijthoff and Noordhoff.

—— (1985) "The science of sentiment: the problem of the cerebral localization of emotion," in P. Bateson and Peter Klopfer (eds) *Perspectives in Ethology* Vol. 6 – "Mechanisms," New York: Plenum Press.

—— (1992) "Afternoon roundtable discussion: Friday, August 3, 1990," in Anne Harrington (ed.) *So Human a Brain: Knowledge and Values in the Neurosciences*, Boston: Birkhäuser, pp. 261–74.

Edelman, Gerald (1992) *Bright Air, Brilliant Fire: On the Matter of Mind*, New York: Basic Books.

Eibl-Eibesfeldt, Irenaus (1970) *Ethology: The Biology of Behavior*, New York: Holt, Reinhart and Winston.

Fisher, Roland (1987) "Emergence of mind from brain: the biological roots of the hermeneutic circle," *Diogenes* 138: 1–25.

Fromm, Eric (1973) *The Anatomy of Human Destructiveness*, Greenwich, CT: Fawcett.

Gaster, G.H. (1958) *The Oldest Stories in the World*, Boston: Beacon.

Gorman, Warren (1960) *Body, Image and Image of the Brain*, St Louis, MO: Warren H. Green.

Hameroff, S. and Penrose, R. (1996) "Orchestrated reduction of quantum coherence in brain microtubules," in S. Hameroff, A. Kaszniak and A. Scott (eds) *Towards a Science of Consciousness*, Cambridge, MA: MIT Press, pp. 507–40.

Harth, Erich (1993) *The Creative Loop: How the Brain Makes a Mind*, Reading, MA: Addison-Wesley.

—— (1996) "Self-referent mechanisms as the neuronal basis of consciousness," in S. Hameroff, A. Kaszniak, and A. Scott (eds) *Toward a Science of Consciousness*, Cambridge, MA: MIT Press, 611–31.

Heidegger, Martin (1971 [1959]) *On the Way to Language*, trans. Peter Hertz, New York: Harper and Row.

Hegel, G.W.F. (1892 [1817]) *The Logic of Hegel*, trans. William Wallace, 2nd edn, Oxford: Oxford University Press.

—— (1969 [1816]) *Hegel's Science of Logic*, trans. A.V. Miller, foreword J.N. Findlay, New York: Humanities Press.

Hesiod (1974) *The Homeric Hymns and Homerica*, trans. Hugh Evelyn-White, Cambridge, MA: Harvard University Press.

Hingston, R. (1933) *The Meaning of Animal Colour and Adornment; Being a New Explanation of the Colours, Adornments and Courtships of Animals, Their Songs, Moults, Extravagant Weapons, the Differences Between Their Sexes, the Manner of Formation of Their Geographical Varieties and Other Allied Problems*, London: Arnold.

Hobson, J. (1994) *The Chemistry of Conscious States: How the Brain Changes its Mind*, Boston, MA: Little, Brown.

Hofstadter, Douglas (1980) *Gödel, Escher, Bach: an Eternal Golden Braid*, New York: Vintage.

Hooker, Richard (1954 [1594]) *Of the Laws of Ecclesiastical Polity*, Vol. 2, intro. Christopher Morris, New York: E.P. Dutton.

Hooper, Judith and Teresi, Dick (1986) *The Three Pound Universe*, New York: Macmillan.

Johnson-Laird, P.N. (1988) "A computational analysis of consciousness," in A. Marcel and E. Bisiach (eds) *Consciousness and Contemporary Science*, New York: Oxford University Press.

Kant, Immanuel (1965 [1787]) *Critique of Pure Reason*, trans. Norman Smith, New York: St Martin's Press.

—— (1968 [1790]) *Critique of Judgement*, trans. Norman Smith, New York: St Martin's Press.

—— (1969 [1785]) *Foundations of the Metaphysics of Morals*, trans. Lewis Beck, R. Wolff (ed.), Indianapolis, IN: Bobbs-Merrill.

Keyes, C. (1973) *God or Ichabod?: A Non-Violent Christian Nihilism*, Cincinnati, OH: Forward Movement.

—— (1989) *Foundations for an Ethic of Dignity: A Study in the Degradation of the Good*, Lewiston, NY: The Edwin Mellen Press.

—— (1991) *New Harvest: Transplanting Body Parts and Reaping the Benefits*, Clifton, NJ: Humana Press.

—— (1992) "Ethical judgement and brain function: an interpretation of Paul D. MacLean's hypothesis," *Journal of Social and Evolutionary Systems* 15(4): 387–98.

—— (1996) "Crisis of brain and self," *Zygon: Journal of Religion and Science* 31 (December): 583–95.

—— (1997) "Paul D. MacLean's triune brain hypothesis: which Platonic metaphor fits and which does not?" *Proceedings of the Institute for Liberal Studies, Science and Culture* 8 (Fall): 18–21.

Kierkegaard, Søren (1959 [1843]) *Either/Or Vol.1*, trans. David Swenson and Lillian Swenson; rev. and foreword Howard Johnson, Princeton, NJ: Princeton University Press.

—— (1992 [1846]) *Concluding Unscientific Postscript to Philosophical Fragments,* Vol. 1, trans. and intro. Howard Hong and Edna Hong (eds), Princeton, NJ: Princeton University Press.

Koestler, Arthur (1967) *The Ghost in the Machine,* London: Hutchinson.

Laughlin, Charles, McManus, M., and d'Aquili, Eugene (1992) *Brain, Symbol, and Experience,* New York: Columbia University Press.

Lewis, C.S. (1965 [1946]) *That Hideous Strength,* New York: Macmillan.

Longinus (1965 [*c.*60]) *On the Sublime,* trans. W. Fyfe, in *Aristotle, The Poetics, "Longinus" On the Sublime, Demetrius On Style,* Cambridge, MA: Harvard University Press.

Lucretius (1932 [*c.*54 BC]) *On the Nature of Things,* trans. and ed. H. Munro, London: G. Bell and Sons.

Luria, A.R. (1972) *The Man With a Shattered World: The History of a Brain Wound,* trans. Lynn Solotaroff, New York: Basic Books.

—— (1973) *The Working Brain: An Introduction to Neuropsychology,* trans. Basil Haigh, New York: Basic Books.

McGinn, Colin (1991) *The Problem of Consciousness,* Oxford: Basil Blackwell.

McKeown, Roy (1980) *Cabin in the Blackjacks: a History of Ada, Oklahoma,* Ada, OK: Roy McKeown.

Macklin, Ruth (1978) "Man's animal brains and animal nature: some implications of a psychophysiological theory," *Philosophy and Phenomenological Research* 39: 155–83.

MacLean, Paul (1949) "Psychosomatic disease and the 'visceral brain,' recent developments bearing on the Papez theory of emotion," *Psychosomatic Medicine* 11: 338–537.

—— (1962) "New findings relevant to the evolution of psychosexual functions of the brain," *Journal of Nervous and Mental Disease* 135: 289–301.

—— (1964) "Man and his animal brains," *Modern Medicine* 32: 95–106.

—— (1985) "Brain evolution relating to family, play, and the separation call," *Archives of General Psychiatry* 42 (April): 405–17.

—— (1990) *The Triune Brain in Evolution,* New York: Plenum.

—— (1992) "Obtaining knowledge of the subjective brain ('epistemics')," in Anne Harrington (ed.) *So Human a Brain: Knowledge and Values in the Neurosciences,* Boston, MA: Birkhäuser, pp. 57–70.

—— (1997) "The brain and subjective experience: questions of multilevel role of resonance," *The Journal of Mind and Behavior* 18 (Spring and Summer): 247 [145]–268 [166].

Makeig, Scott (1982) "Affective versus analytic perception of musical intervals," in Manfred Clynes and Janice Walker (eds) *Music, Mind, and Brain: The Neuropsychology of Music,* New York: Plenum Press, pp. 227–50.

Mark, Vernon and Ervin, Frank (1970) *Violence and the Brain,* New York: Houghton Mifflin Company.

Mayer, André and Wheeler, Michael (1982) *The Crocodile Man: A Case of Brain Chemistry and Criminal Violence,* New York: Houghton Mifflin Company.

Miller, G. (1971) *Moral and Ethical Implications of Human Organ Transplants,* Springfield, IL: Charles L. Thomas.

Morris, D. (1967) *The Naked Ape,* New York: McGraw Hill.

Mueller, Gustav (1944) *The World as Spectacle,* New York: Philosophical Library.

Nagel, Thomas (1974) "What is it like to be a bat?" *Philosophical Review* 83: 435–50.
—— (1986) *The View From Nowhere*, New York: Oxford University Press.
Nietzsche, Friedrich (1967 [1872]) *The Birth of Tragedy and the Case of Wagner*, trans. and comm. Walter Kaufmann, New York: Vintage.
Otto, Rudolf (1969 [1917]) *The Idea of the Holy*, trans. John Harvey, New York: Oxford University Press.
Ovid (1976 [*c.* 8]) *Metamorphoses*, Vol. 2, trans. Frank Miller, Cambridge, MA: Harvard University Press.
Oxford English Dictionary, The (1989) 2nd edn, prepared by J.A. Simpson and E.S.C. Weiner, vol. 14, Oxford: Clarendon Press.
Peele, Talmage (1977) *The Neuroanatomic Basis for Clinical Neurology*, New York: McGraw Hill.
Penrose, Roger (1994) *Shadows of the Mind: A Search for the Missing Science of Consciousness*, New York: Oxford University Press.
Peterson, Steven (1983) "The psychobiology of hypostatizing," *Micropolitics* 2 (4): 423–51.
—— (1988) "Human ethology and political hierarchy: is democracy feasible?" paper prepared for presentation at conference on Biology and the Prospects for Democracy, Villa Vigoni, Menaggio, Italy, 24–26 November 1988.
Plato (1892) *Symposium*, in *The Dialogues of Plato*, 3rd edn, trans. B. Jowett, New York: Oxford University Press.
—— (1951) *Phaedo*, trans. F. Church, Indianapolis, IN: Bobbs-Merrill.
—— (1968) *The Republic*, trans., intro., and notes Allan Bloom, New York: Basic Books.
—— (1972) *Phaedrus*, trans. and intro. R. Hackforth, Cambridge: Cambridge University Press.
—— (1975) *Timaeus*, trans. R. Bury, Cambridge, MA: Harvard University Press.
Powers, William (1980) "A systems approach to consciousness," in Richard Davidson and Julian Davidson (eds) *Psychobiology of Consciousness*, New York: Plenum Press, pp. 217–42.
Pribram, Carl (1982) "Brain mechanism in music: prolegomena for a theory of the meaning of music," in Manfred Clynes and Janice Walker (eds) *Music, Mind, and Brain: the Neuropsychology of Music*, New York: Plenum Press, 21–36.
Ricoeur, Paul (1967) *The Sybolism of Evil*, trans. Emerson Buchanan, Boston, MA: Beacon Press.
Roederer, Juan (1982) "Physical and neuropsychological foundations of music: the basic questions," in Manfred Clynes and Janice Walker (eds) *Music, Mind, and Brain: the Neuropsychology of Music*, New York: Plenum Press, pp. 37–46.
Sagan, Carl (1977) *The Dragons of Eden: Speculations on the Evolution of Human Intelligence*, New York: Random House.
—— (1980) *Cosmos*, New York: Random House.
Schwartz, G.E. (1980) Foreword to Richard Davidson and Julian Davidson (eds) *Psychobiology of Consciousness*, New York: Plenum Press.
Scott, Alwyn (1995) *Stairway to the Mind: the Controversial New Science of Consciousness*, New York: Springer-Verlag.
Siodmak, Curt (1943) *Donovan's Brain*, New York: Putnam Books.
Snyder, Soloman (1978) "Opiate receptors and morphine-like peptides," *Harvey Lectures* 73: 291–314.

Sun Tzu (1971) *The Art of War*, trans. Samuel Griffith, New York: Oxford University Press.

Tillich, Paul (1952) *The Courage to Be*, New Haven, CT: Yale University Press.

Uttal, W. (1988) *On Seeing Forms*, Hillsdale, NJ: L. Erlbaum Associates.

Velmans, Max (ed.) (1996) *The Science of Consciousness: Psychological, Neuropsychological and Clinical Reviews*, New York: Routledge.

Washburn, S. and Lancaster, L. (1993) "Evolution of hunting," in Russell Ciochon and John Fleagle (eds) *The Human Evolution Sourcebook*, Englewood Cliffs, NJ: Prentice Hall.

Watson, John (1924) *Behaviourism*, New York: The People's Institute.

White, Robert, Albin, J., Verdua, J., and Locke, G. (1967) "The isolated monkey's brain: operative preparation and design of support system," *Journal of Neurosurgery* 27: 216–25.

Williston, S.W. (1925) *The Osteology of the Reptiles*, Cambridge, MA: Harvard University Press.

Wolf, George (1984) "The place of the brain in an ocean of feelings," in John Cobb Jr and Franklin Gamvell (eds) *Existence and Actuality: Conversations with Charles Hartshorne*, Chicago: University of Chicago Press, pp. 167–84.

Zigas, Vincent (1990) *The Laughing Death: The Untold Story of Kuru*, Clifton, NJ: Humana Press.

Index